Contents

A Phoenix Study Guide

Written By

ROSELLE THOMPSON

For the text

EAGLE PUBLICATIONS

Published by Eagle Publications
P O Box 73374, London W3 3FZ, England.

A Paperback Original
First published in Great Britain in 2015

Cover design by V3Creative Designs

ISBN 978-0-9542325-8-0

A CIP catalogue record for this book is available from the British Library

Printed in Great Britain by IngramSpark
Paper used by Eagle Publications books are made from wood grown in sustainable forests.

www.eaglepublications.co.uk

Getting the most from - *A Woman of Destiny*

The book is about Joanne, the W*oman of Destiny,* who sets off on a quest to find her absent father from Grenada to England. It presents both a personal and historical narrative that projects Joanne's experiences as part of the British-Caribbean migrant story; as it focuses on her life with her families in Grenada, as well as in England. The novel provides an account of those issues which help to build Joanne's resilience, in order to fulfill her destiny. Through these issues we are also presented with an account of Grenadian family life in the region during the late 1960's, to a period of migration that saw many families leaving the Caribbean for the First World e.g. Britain, Canada and USA, and continuing in a steady flow with their children into the 1990's. However, the settings of **this book's actions take place solely in Grenada and West London**.

Key facts

Title: ***A Woman of Destiny: A Calypso Novel***

Author: Roselle Thompson

Type of work: Novel

Genre: Calypso Novel & Historical fiction

Language: English (with Grenadian Creole and idiomatic expressions)

Time & Place written: UK 2014

Date of first publication: December 2014

Publisher: Eagle Publications

Narrator: At first the narrator is a child and is part of the Grenadian community but later she migrates to England, at the age of 13 where she grows up. However, as narrator, she also presents a collective consciousness and speaks with a communal voice.

Climax: The climax of the central plot occurs when Joanne discovers that, contrary to what she had thought, she was not so much an unwanted child but was deliberately robbed of a paternal relationship that could have been; so decides to curtail the search for her father. Instead, she becomes self-directed and determined to be an independent thinker; selective of aspects of her tradition and positive towards her future. However, the novel's many digressions and movements back and forth in time and place, offer not only the main narrative, which is Joanne's story, but also many alternative climaxes, achieved via sub-characters in the novel.

Protagonist: Joanne, Gran-gran, Aunt Meena

Antagonists: This depends on the reader's perspectives: the unfulfilled Justin's dad; the cuckolded Sukram; the 'African priest'; those against the Calypso/carnival tradition are possible characters.

Settings (time): late 1960 to the late 1990's

Settings (place): Grenadian village in the Parish of St. Andrews (specifically the village in Gutt), and Britain, (specifically Ealing, West London).

Point of view: the point of view shifts throughout the novel but it is primarily that of the master-narrator, with subtle 'interjections' from Calypsos/Calypsonians at the beginning of each Chapter.

Narrative Style: The novel is narrated in a flashback style. Information is revealed via the "I" persona with Joanne's story; when we are either told things about various characters in the novel or from the characters themselves. Joanne also overhears information from adults' conversations. She is a commentator on the behaviour of others in the novel, and of the wider situation in Grenada.

Musically, the novel deliberately mirrors the music of the novel's sub-title. Various characters "*improvising;*" presenting *solo, duo, trio and quartet* as well as group percussionist compositions that fit together to create a whole book/composition. The tone of the novel shifts with Joanne's *solo composition*, which is the main story in the novel. This is joined by other compositions from other characters. Many of the elements are the folksy, jovial, carnivalesque rhythms, lament, remembering, regret - reflective of the *blues*, *gospelypso*; the *call-and-response* techniques (from the church services); to the sensual *ballads* of would-be successful relationships.

Tense: The narrative tense in the novel alternates between past and present tense, using flashback techniques.

Foreshadowing: The novel's structure ***(Prologue- Part I & Epilogue - Part II)***, spells out a cycle of movements of migrants from one landscape (Caribbean to the other and vice versa, in death), leaving little surprise in the story time-line which suggests that both beginning and end are the same. Joanne's quest for information, whether by direct conversation, being tutored by friends, eavesdropping, or overhearing information; foreshadows her search for her father, as well as the possibility of a partner.

Tones: Grenadian vernaculars, with colloquial language, fused with French Creole; familiar; musical; rhythmic; associative; universal; stream-of-consciousness.

Themes: migration, music, storytelling, memory, childhood innocence and experience, religion, adolescence, gossip, sexual exploitation, death, matriarchy, violence, tragedy, *obeah*, love, post-independence blues, tradition and culture, men's destiny, corruption, linguistic fusions, landscape & identity, race, motherhood/fatherhood, superstition, nationhood, determination, fused generic techniques, destiny/empowerment and Diaspora.

Symbols: landscape, narrator's story, the quest

A Woman of Destiny – A Historical Context

The Context of this Study Guide provides information on the historical, cultural and literary background of *A Woman of Destiny: A Calypso Novel.* Your insights into *A Woman of Destiny* will be much sharper if you understand the place and period the novel was set in. The context will have an effect on the events in the novel, and this will help you to understand the text.

The historical context is important because the time in history that the text is written will affect the way the characters behave, speak and think. In addition, the cultural context will present the culture of its society, traditions and even the Author's background may have an effect on the writing. In other words, this Study Guide provides information that shows you the "big picture" and enhances your enjoyment of the novel so that you will be able to answer the following questions.

- **What has happened in Grenada in the last 30 years or so?**
- **Why are the characters leaving Grenada for England?**
- **Why is there a mixture of spoken Grenadian language styles?**
- **What is a Calypso and how does it function in the novel?**
- **What is the Diaspora?**
- **What is Thompson's background?**
- **What is '*Destiny*' and what influenced the writing of *A Woman of Destiny*?**

Isle of Spice: Nutmegs - www.gov.gd

The State of Grenada, (pronounced gre-nay-da) consists of three islands - **Grenada, Carriacou and Petite Martinique** which form the southern end of the Windward Islands. Grenada is at the southern end of the Grenadines in the southeastern Caribbean Sea. It is located northwest of Trinidad & Tobago, northeast of Venezuela, and southwest of St. Vincent and the Grenadines.

Grenada is also known as the "*Island of Spice*" because of the production of nutmeg and mace crops of which Grenada is one of the world's largest exporters. Its size is 344 square kilometres (133 sq ml), with an estimated population of 110,000. The capital of Grenada is St. Georges.

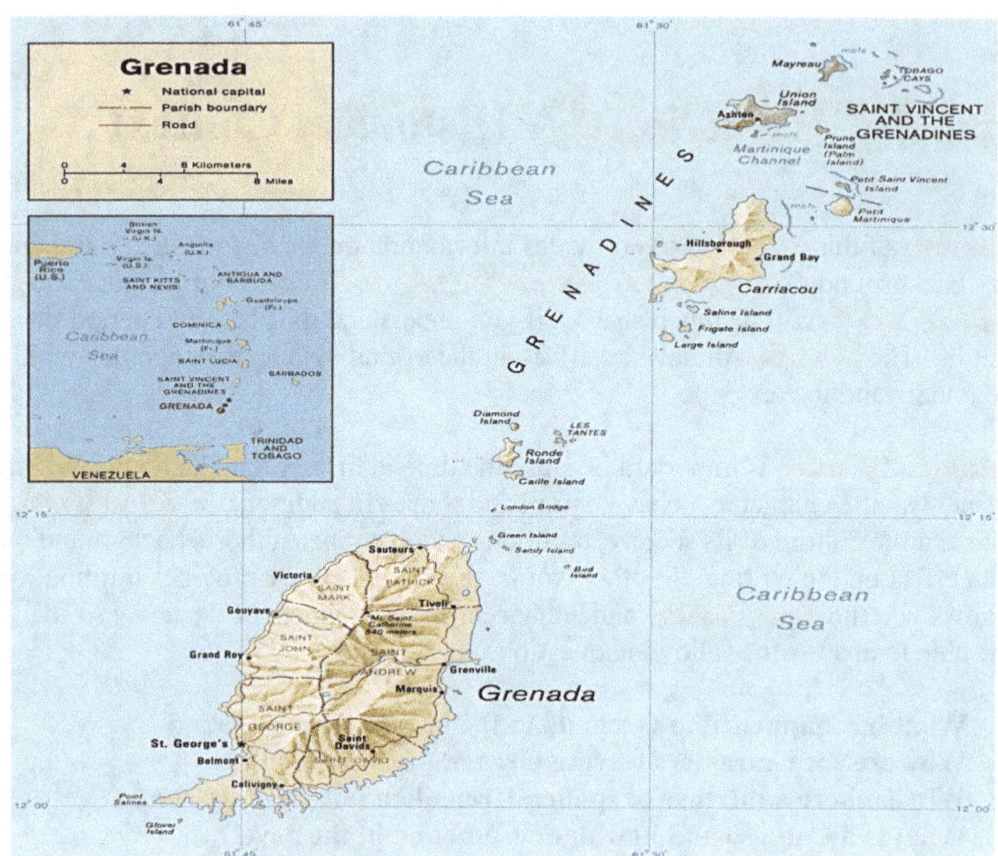

Grenada as mentioned in the Novel
www.lib.utexas.edu/maps/americas.htm

Grenada was French colony for 114 years – (1649–1763)

On **17th March 1649, a French expedition of 203 men from Martinique, led by Jacques du Parquet, founded a permanent settlement on Grenada.** This led to conflict with **the indigenous islanders, (who were Amerindians - *Caribs and Arawaks*)**, which lasted **until 1654**, when the island was completely ruled by the French. **The French named the new French Colony *La Grenade*.** They established a capital known as Fort Royal, (which later became known as **St. George**). **Some of the surviving Amerindians either fled to neighboring islands such as Dominica, St. Vincent and the Grenadines**, or retreated to remoter parts of Grenada during the 1700s. The economy at that time was initially based on sugar cane and indigo. However, following a period of Seven Years' War, **the British captured Grenada from the French in 1762**.

Grenada – was a British colony for 211 years - (1763–1974)

Grenada was formally ceded to Britain by the *Treaty of Paris* in 1763. The French recaptured the island during the American War of Independence, after Comte d'Estaing won the bloody land and naval Battle of Grenada in July 1779. However, **the island was restored to Britain with the *Treaty of Versailles* in 1783.** Britain was hard pressed to overcome a pro-French revolt in 1795–1796 led by Julien Fedon. In **1877, Grenada was made a *Crown Colony***. **Theophilus A. Marryshow** founded the ***Representative Government Association*** (RGA) in 1917 to agitate for a new and participative constitutional dispensation for the Grenadian people.

Moving Toward independence (1950–1974)

In **1950, Eric Matthew Gairy founded the Grenada United Labour Party (GULP),** initially as a trades union, which led the 1951general strike for better working conditions. This sparked great unrest—so many buildings were set ablaze that the disturbances became known as the 'red sky' days—and the British Authorities had to call in military reinforcements to help regain control of the situation. **On October 10, 1951, Grenada held its first general elections on the basis of universal adult suffrage, with Gairy's party winning six of the eight seats contested.** **From 1958 to 1962 Grenada was part of the Federation of the West Indies.** **On March 3, 1967, Grenada was granted full autonomy over its internal affairs as an Associated State.**

Independence and revolution (1974–1983)

Independence was granted in 1974 under the leadership of Eric Gairy, who became the **first Prime Minister of Grenada**. Civil conflict gradually broke out between Eric Gairy's government and some opposition parties including the New Jewel Movement (NJM). Gairy's party won elections in 1976, but the opposition did not accept the result, accusing it of fraud. **In 1979, the New Jewel Movement, under Maurice Bishop, launched a paramilitary attack on the government resulting in its overthrow.**

Coup and execution of Maurice Bishop

Some **years later, a dispute** developed between Bishop and certain high-ranking members of the NJM. Though Bishop cooperated with Cuba and the USSR on various trade and foreign policy issues, he sought to maintain a "non-aligned" status. **Bishop had been taking his time making Grenada wholly socialist, encouraging private-sector development in an attempt to make the island a popular tourist destination.** On **October 19, 1983**, **Bernard Coard and his wife Phyllis, backed by the Grenadian Army, led a coup against the government of Maurice Bishop and placed Bishop under house arrest.** He was eventually freed after street demonstrations in the capital. **When Bishop attempted to resume power, he was captured and executed by soldiers along with seven others,** including government cabinet ministers.

Invasion by the United States

On **October 25, 1983**, combined forces from the **United States** and from the Regional Security System (RSS) based in Barbados, **invaded Grenada** in an operation codenamed Operation Urgent Fury. **Reagan was worried that Cuba – under the direction of the Soviet Union – would use Grenada as a refueling stop for Cuban and Soviet airplanes loaded with weapons destined for Central American communist insurgents. Bishop had stated the purpose of the airstrip was for an airport,** to allow commercial jets to land. The U.S. stated this was done following requests from Prime Minister Eugenia Charles of Dominica and the Governor-General of Grenada, Sir Paul Scoon. **The United Nations General Assembly condemned it as "a flagrant violation of international law" by a vote of 108 in favor to 9, with 27 abstentions.**

Post-invasion arrests

After the invasion of the island nation, the pre-revolutionary Grenadian constitution came into operation once again. **Eighteen members of the PRG and the PRA (army) were arrested after the invasion on charges related to the murder of Maurice Bishop** and seven others. The eighteen included the top political leadership of Grenada at the time of the execution as well as the entire military chain of command directly responsible for the operation that led to the executions. **Fourteen were sentenced to death**, one was found **not guilty and three were sentenced to forty-five years in prison**. The death sentences were eventually commuted to terms of imprisonment. **Those in prison have become known as the "Grenada 17."**

Grenada since 1983

When U.S. troops withdrew from Grenada in December 1983, **Nicholas Brathwaite** of the National Democratic Congress was appointed prime minister of an interim administration by **Sir Paul Scoon** until elections could be organized. The first democratic elections since 1976 were held in December 1984 and were won by the Grenada National Party under **Herbert Blaize** who served as prime minister until his death in December 1989. **Ben Jones** succeeded Blaize as prime minister and served until the March 1990 election, which was won by the National Democratic Congress under **Nicholas Brathwaite** who returned as prime minister for a second time until he resigned in February 1995. He was succeeded by **George Brizan** who served until the June 1995 election which was won by the New National Party under **Keith Mitchell** who went on to win the **1999** and **2003** elections and served for a record 13 years until **2008** and then again in **2013**. **Keith Mitchell is currently the Prime Minister of Grenada.**

Colonialism

It is obvious when looking at the history of Grenada that the island was in the grip of colonialism for a considerable amount of time. Beginning with the sixteenth century, **colonial masters, (in Grenada's case - British and French)**, travelled the world extensively, and taking lands as colonies, for two main reasons. **The colonies had**

resources such as valuable crops e.g. sugarcane, cocoa, spices and cheap labour, which helped to make Britain wealthy. Other islands were of use because of their strategic positions and were used as bases for military action.

Although the British Empire was the largest in the world, other **European colonisers colonised countries in the Caribbean region, e.g. France (Grenada); Spain (Jamaica); Holland (Guyana).** Therefore, the fact that these colonisers also had colonies in Africa made it easy for them to transport African slaves to plantations in the Caribbean region to extract wealth from the colonies and transport it to Britain. In fact, these Colonisers traded colonies amongst themselves, by selling them or handing over, as part of a treaty, after a war. **Notice that in Grenada's case, the island was formally ceded to Britain from French rule by the *Treaty of Paris in 1763*** and later, the island was **restored to Britain with the *Treaty of Versailles in 1783***.

In ***A Woman of Destiny,* the narrator talks of the state of political and cultural affairs in Grenada, at a time of the fading era of British colonialism and the approaching advent of independence of the island from Britain.** We see the young children grappling with issues to do with relics of colonialism in the meaningless rousing British war-time songs that were sung; Mr. Jessup, the Headmaster's military style drilling of pupils in school; the content of the curriculum with Wordsworth, Blake, Shakespeare; the existence of the Union Jack and the prominence of the Queen's portrait in the school; all represent structures of colonial dominance in the island.

As with most colonies after the Second World War, rather than seen as assets, British colonies became an economic burden to Britain. In addition many Caribbean islands agitated and lobbied Britain for self-rule and were granted independence from the 1960's onwards. **In Grenada's case, the approaching independence mentioned in *A Woman of Destiny,* was the period leading up to 1974.** Independence would mean installing a government of local people who would govern with independence but with a British style democracy, fair elections, parliaments and a Privy Council.

The narrator in ***A Woman of Destiny*** talks of **everyone in the island being given an opportunity to compete and write their own versions of a national anthem for independence.** This sense of island-wide participation is reflective of a style of democracy, and suggests individual freedom to participate and a sense of self-determination. This image is in direct contrast to the image of dominion, seen up to this point by structures, (as mentioned above); set up to perpetuate colonial rule in the island.

Since independence, few Caribbean people have questioned the morality of colonialism in the region but exceptions such as the Grenadian-born Professor Gus John, born 11 March 1945, writer, campaigner, lecturer, and education consultant, refused to accept a CBE (*Commander of the Order of the British Empire*), offered to him in the Queen's New Year Honours List, 2000.

Prof. John refused the Empire medal on the basis that he regarded the title, 'Commander of the British Empire', as part of the iconography of British imperialism. Prof John states that, *"One of the major impediments to promoting racial equality is the legacy of empire. I believe the whole thing is iniquitous."* [1] In other words, he felt it would be a dishonour to accept his award as a 'Commander' of the very institution he had tried to demolish.

In ***A Woman of Destiny*, Justin's dad, the Grenadian fictional character boasts about his colonial education. He is able to recite Wordsworth, Keats and Shelley** and speaks admiringly about his mastery of Standard English, with reference to **etymology, phonology, syntax, and prosody; though they cause "*confusion*"** in his head. However, he does not view working on the land, associated with his ancestral past e.g. slavery, slave labour, as a way forward or as social, economic and educational advancement. **He does stress the primacy of "*the book,*" which represents aspects of colonialism** he prefers, when he publicly instructs his son to take the literary route, as a fillip towards his **'*destiny*'**.

Working on the land is therefore seen as aspects of a past to be rejected profusely. Later, we are disconcerted when he challenges the young narrator, as she strives to write her version of the National Anthem for the coming independent event in the island. Justin's dad is surprisingly quite harsh with Joanne, when he crushes her spirit, belittles her, openly challenges her. Furthermore, he is callous with his prediction that she will not be able to pass an exam. Surprisingly, as someone who appears to be pro-education, he reduces the girl to a tearful, deflated wreck without a slightest thought of the consequences.

In a sense, in ***A Woman of Destiny***, **Justin's dad is a victim of colonialism; not being really British (other than technically a citizen of a former colony; which would entitle him to a British passport),** he is not fully acceptant of aspects of his Grenadian cultural tradition, and this could account for the fact that **is a tragic figure** in many ways.

Politics

As a Commonwealth realm, **Queen Elizabeth II is Queen of Grenada and Head of State.** The Crown is represented by a Governor-General, currently Cécile La Grenade. Day-to-day executive power lies with the **Head of Government, the Prime Minister**. Although appointed by the Governor-General, the Prime Minister is **usually the leader of the largest party in the Parliament.**

The Parliament consists of a Senate (thirteen members) and a House of Representatives (fifteen members). The senators are appointed by the government and the opposition, while the representatives are elected by the population for five-year terms.

On February 19, 2013, Prime Minister Keith Claudius Mitchell 65, led the New National Party (NNP) to victory with a clean sweep of 15 seats. **Mitchell** was sworn into office on February 21 and is the country's **ninth prime minister since it attained political independence from Britain in 1974.**

Demographics

A majority of Grenadians **(at least 80%),** are **descendants of the African Slaves brought by the English and French**; few of the **indigenous Carib and Arawak** population survived the French purge at Sateurs (in St. Patrick Parish). A small percentage of descendants of indentured workers from India were brought to Grenada mainly from the North Indian states of Bihar and Uttar Pradesh, between May 1, 1857 – January 10, 1885. Today, Grenadians of **Indian descent comprise the second largest ethnic group**. There is also a small community of **French and English descendants**. The rest of the population (**13%) is of mixed races**.

Migration

Grenada, like many of the Caribbean islands is subject to a large amount of migration, with a large number of young people wanting to leave the island to seek life elsewhere. With **110,000 people living in Grenada**, estimates and census data suggest that there are at least that number of Grenadian-born people in other parts of the Caribbean (such as Barbados and Trinidad) and **at least that number again in First World countries**. Popular migration points for Grenadians further north include New York, Toronto, Montreal, the United Kingdom (especially London and the Midlands e.g. Yorkshire), and Australia.

Religion

European and Canadian missionaries took Christianity to Grenada. Their strategy was to run schools and holiday activities for children, to ensure that as converts, the children absorbed the Christian message. In ***A Woman of Destiny*** Joanne, experiences this when Miss Gisbreth arrives on the island during the children's holidays. Also the incident with the *"African priest"* shows how misguided missionary zeal could ruin children, when it was revealed that their guest was neither an African nor a priest.

Apart from a small community of Rastafarians living in Grenada, **most of the population belongs to Christian churches. About half of the population is Roman Catholic,** while the largest Protestant denomination is Anglican, with Presbyterian and Seventh Day Adventist taking up much of the remainder. In ***A Woman of Destiny*** the narrator's family members are **Baptists, who are a small section of the religious denominations**. Unlike this group, most churches have denomination-based schools but are open to all.

The narrator in ***A Woman of Destiny*** and her best friend go to an Anglican school and they join other school children travelling on a bus to a nearby Catholic Convent school run by nuns.

There are **small Hindu and Muslim populations**, descended mostly **from Gujarati Indian immigrants** who came during the colonial period and set up merchant shops. Therefore, these are vestiges of these influences which form part of the cultural tradition.

What is interesting about **Joanne's family's church is that their style of worship is akin to African religious styles.** In *A Woman of Destiny,* the narrator describes Mother Sayee ringing bells in four corners and writing inscriptions with chalk on the ground. There is a suggestion of a kind of **fusion of Africanism with Christianity** that informs the style of worship.

Traditionally, there **seems to be more preference for the Catholic religion** because in *A Woman of Destiny,* Joanne tells us as they appear to attract more people and their buildings are bigger. However, the **kinder face of religion is presented by Joanne's Gran-gran,** who ensures that Joanne's reading skills are developed, as she takes "Comfort" from her ***"Words of Comfort;"*** which really are passages from the Bible. Some people live strict, religious lives, as Joanne's family does. They shut out the outside world, including the local tradition (carnival), until this seemed a mockery, with the resulting "*African priest's*" deceit. Others prefer the alternative, and are not interested in religion; preferring to seek the rum shop and partaking in their own brand of 'communion' with the island's finest rum.

Language & Culture

English is the country's official language of Grenada, but the main spoken language is either of two **English-based Creole languages** (**Grenadian Creole English and Grenadian Creole French**); which reflect the **Indian, African, and European heritage** of the nation. These Creole languages contain elements from a variety of **African languages** and **Grenadian French Creole** or **French patois** (pronounced *pat-wa*); is influenced by the French language. However, the **French Patois sometimes also referred to as Antillean Creole, is also spoken by about 10-20% of the population.**

Grenadian Creole French or **Kwéyòl** is mainly known as **Patois** (pronounced *pat-wa*). This language is mainly spoken in smaller rural areas, but today it can only be heard in a few small pockets of the society. It is for this reason that in ***A Woman of Destiny***, Gran-gran and her contemporaries' language consists of a mixture of **Grenadian French Patois** and **Grenadian Creole English**. They have the privilege of being able to **speak two languages** and this is why **the older generation**, represented by Gran-gran, is able to speak **Grenadian French Patois** and shut the children out from their conversation.

Other influences in the island are evidenced by some **Hindi/Bhojpuri terms** which are still spoken amongst the Indian descendants; mostly those related to the kitchen; such as ***aloo, geera, kareila, seim, chownkay, and baylay***. The term ***bhai***, which means '***brother***' in Urdu and Hindi, is a common form of greeting amongst Indo-Grenadian males of equal status.

In *A Woman of Destiny*, Joanne tells us that she understands the *Creole French* and responds to this in communication with her Grandmother but at no time do we see her speaking the Creole French. Therefore, it is the preserve of those whose lives were impacted on by French rule and later British colonialism. It is for this reason that the

everyday language is laced with French words or patois and the **local Creole dialect**. This is borne out by the **language used by the older women** in ***A Woman of Destiny***. It suggests a movement between the two political eras; confirming the island's social and political reality. By contrast, in ***A Woman of Destiny*** Joanne and the children of the village were born during the period of British domination of the island, when English was the official language of government and education. Therefore, having been educated entirely in English, they are speakers of Standard English and the Grenada Creole English. In ***A Woman of Destiny,*** there is no indication that Gran-gran went to school or has been taught to read and write, but it is clear that she has a love for the book-form.

Today, French influence on Grenadian culture is much less visible, compared with other Caribbean islands, surnames and place names in French remain. (e.g. ***La Poutrie, Grand Anse, La Sagesse, La Bay, Sauteurs, Point Salines, Petit Bacaye, Morne Fendue, L'Anse Aux Epines).*** Also a stronger French influence is found in the well-seasoned spicy food and styles of cooking similar to those found in New Orleans, and some French architecture has survived from the 1700s. **Grenada's culture is heavily influenced by the African roots of most of the Grenadian, but Indian and Carib Amerindian influence is also seen with dhal puri, rotis, Indian sweets, cassava and curries in the cuisine.**

Calypso, Soca and reggae musical genres set the mood for Grenada's annual Carnival activities. The main characteristic of the Calypso is the significance of its oral transmission. Communication is realized through face-to-face contact with a live audience and singer. **The song is presented by a Calypsonian/singer,** who functions as a person whose job it is to, not only **sing joyous songs**, but ***"tell it like it is."*** This means sing about every aspect of society, whether good, bad or indifferent: (*See separate section on the significance of Calypso in the novel for more details).* However, over the years, other musical forms such as **rap music**, **became famous among Grenadian youths,** and there have been numerous young rappers emerging in the island's underground rap scene. **Zouk** is also being slowly introduced onto the island from neighbouring countries. **The islanders' African and Carib Amerindian heritage plays an influential role** in many aspects of Grenada's culture.

www.mightysparrow.com

Timeline

1960	PART I	
NOVEL STARTS HERE Chapters 1, 2, 3, 4, 5, 6, 7, 8	GRENADA	The Funeral of the Caribbean/Grenadian returnee
		The fight between Jean and Dessima
		Sukram's murder and the ensuing drama
		Mark's death – a village in mourning
		Verna, Christopher and the fiasco in England
		The dilemmas of immigrant Grenadians in Britain
		The Man-of-words at the narrator's Farewell
		Grenada's approaching Independence
		The English Headmaster's brand of corporal punishment
		The village children's innocent discussions based on hear-say
		The Corrupt "*African priest*" - the castor oil purge and the women's curses
		Gossiping and family dilemmas about pregnant unwed daughters
		Preparing for The Queen and the Duke's visit to the Caribbean region
Grenada_parishes_named.png		The fathers who don't look after their children and the mothers who 'father' them
1969	**PART II**	
Chapters 9, 10, 11, 12, 13	ENGLAND *Spring*	Joanne migrates to England
		Joanne meets "new family"
		Joanne's "quiet, solemn days"
		Finding a school for Joanne
		The mother's experiences at work in England
		Calvin's unemployment and Joanne's mum dilemma
		The West Country holiday experiences of the youth in England
NOVEL ENDS HERE 1990		The migrant women's dilemma – disappointment and failures
		The quest faded
		Joanne's loneliness & mother's death Joanne's mum - Return to Grenada for burial

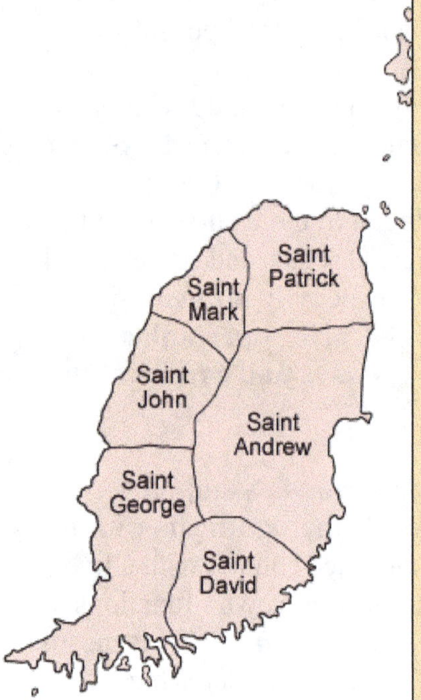

Roselle Thompson

Thompson was born in Grenada and immigrated to England in 1969. Thompson grew up in a village in St. Andrews, North West of the island, the first of 5 children. She went to primary school and had just begun secondary school when she joined her parents in England. She finished her schooling in England and graduated with B.A Hons in English, MPhil in Literature and has pursued a PhD in Literature.

At a young age Thompson demonstrated her literary prowess when she came first in a *Young Black Writers* competition. She has spent many years researching Caribbean culture (Trinidad, St. Lucia, Guyana, Barbados, Jamaica, Belize, Brazil); via its traditional cultures and literature.

Her unpublished research dissertations, *An Introduction to Caribbean Orature* and also *Understanding the Development of Caribbean Orature: Its Impact on Anglo-Caribbean Writing* have dealt extensively with **Caribbean Orature**, which she advocates, is a new generic reality within the Caribbean canon.

Thompson was brought up in the Baptist faith as Joanne the narrator, in the novel. But later in England, she took to other religions (e.g. Methodist and Pentecostal) from choice, and has also explored Eastern religions. Her understanding of religion and its impact on the individual underpins her stance at the end of the novel, when the character Joanne leaves the graveside in the **Epilogue**, to become self-determined, and independent in her thinking; vowing to take on only aspects of the tradition which she views as relevant to her life.

Thompson is a literary expert with extensive knowledge in education delivery and education management; having headed schools in Britain. She has undertaken many activities outside of the Caribbean region, advocating and highlighting the importance of understanding Caribbean culture for migrants and their families in the Diaspora. She writes across various literary genres; producing Poetry, Short Stories, a Play and non-fiction texts. ***A Woman of Destiny: A Calypso Novel*** is her first full-length fiction work published in 2014.

What does the novel title "*A Woman of Destiny*" means?

The first time we see an emotional connection between Joanne and her mother is during her parting comments, as the mother prepares to leave Grenada bound for England. Her expressed wish is for Joanne to ***"have a destiny,"* (p.29).** The meaning of the word ***"destiny"*** for Joanne's mother and later for the village folks can be translated as expecting ***something good, fortunate and extraordinary to happen to Joanne that characterizes and ensures her future success.***

From a wider frame of reference, *destiny* is a shared success, meaning that Joanne's success will ultimately be adopted by everyone who is connected with her, as also being their personal success as well. The washing of the child, ***"the last quick care,"* (p.39)** though performed as a "duty", could symbolize a form of purification/cleansing, in preparation for the child's eventual claim to her destiny.

The dominant, and recurring motif throughout the novel, is the prediction by the narrator's grandmother and those around her that Joanne will become ***A Woman of Destiny***. This means their prediction is for Joanne to become a very successful person; whose life will reflect all that they have not achieved but wanted for themselves. Several villagers empower Joanne to become ***A Woman of Destiny;*** beginning with Reverend Blackman in the **Prologue.** Therefore, secondary characters, being members of the village as a whole, have a part to play in helping Joanne as she grows, to become that ***"woman of destiny."***

Joanne's grandmother does not only project this destination of success for her but she empowers Joanne by discipleship, making her learn to be observant when she points out those she regards as successful role-models for Joanne to emulate. She also ensures that Joanne takes up all opportunities which she believes will prepare the girl for the projected ***"destiny"*** she envisions.

In Joanne's farewell event in **Chapter 8**, as she prepares to leave the island, Gran-gran is quite pellucid with what she regards the characteristics of being ***A Woman of Destiny*** entails; her projection for Joanne's future. In this Chapter, after all the expressed good wishes from villagers, we see Gran-gran having the last say, as the farewell ends; with her own string of advice and emotional farewell to Joanne. Gran-gran goes through great lengths to explain the essence of what being ***A Woman of Destiny*** entails and does so incisively, beyond mere expression.

1. Being *a woman of destiny* has its characteristics in being **tenacious;** fighting for what you want, *"Sometimes you have to fight hard to get your way in things*
2. Gran-gran refers to **strength** as a pre-requisite to being *a woman of destiny* which must be unsurpassable, as the example she gives is the Ashanti warrior – Joanne's great-grand mother: "*My mother was a strong woman. She did never give up."*
3. She refers to the vital part to be placed by **memory** and actively remembering: *"Remember the mortar and the pestle. Be like them."*

4. Also she advices to **remain unchanging,** and endorses being **steadfast** rather *"like the mortar and pestle,"* whose presence demonstrates staying-power across the generations.
5. She tells Joanne to **refuse to be dominated or suppressed** and gives her instructions as to what strategy to adopt should things go wrong: *"Don't let anyone keep you down. If you fall, rise again."*
6. **Advocating pragmatism**, Gran-gran tells the young girl, *"Never let your heart be troubled."*
7. Finally, Joanne is instructed on the kind of practical action she is required to take with the beads which Gran-gran gives her; (previously belonging to Joanne's great grandmother); since she is sure that as a would-be *woman of destiny,* Joanne will need some form of external support. Therefore, **use of the beads** ensures **a point of contact** since, ***focusing** on them will help you **dry your tears** and **lift you** up in times of sadness. They will **bring joy** when you have sorrow."*

Gran-gran is a seasoned, 70 year old, whose life has been very eventful. Therefore, she does not look at life through rose-tinted glasses, or suggest that all will be well. Instead, she is quite down-to-earth and honest in the advice and instructions she gives the young Joanne, about the expected twists and turns as she meanders through her life path.

St. Georges Market, St. Georges, Grenada.
Courtesy of: Grenadaexplorer.com

Men and Destiny in the novel

Justin's Dad

In contrast to Joanne's managed route to achieving her ***destiny***, **Justin's dad who struggles hard against his own shortcomings, talks to his son about the *destiny* he expects of him - becoming a lawyer,** since his childhood friend in America has achieved this status. Justin's dad, like the members of the village, although simple in their expressions, seem to have a complex mind-set. Being the products of colonial education, they have not progressed much beyond a simple life and day-to-day survival. This is why they envision great success for their children or those who can, migrate to seek betterment abroad.

Justin's dad's *destiny* was curtailed by his forced marriage to Jessica at an early age, so he is regularly drunk. However, he considers others around him to be ***"rum-heads and vagabonds,"* (p.49)** and does not include himself in those he castigates. Instead, he advocates a tenacious engagement with **"books," (p.50).** He equates educational success for his son as having a double function: Justin's success will also symbolically be his success too.

Calvin

However, it is possible to see Justin's dad's struggles in the Caribbean environment as a foreshadowing of the difficulties Calvin encounters in England. Whereas Justin's dad's *destiny* was curtailed by his unplanned and forced marriage to Jessica, **Calvin's *destiny* appears neutered by circumstances also but from the prevailing situation in England and in his household.** He has expressed ambitions of becoming a solicitor but his menial employment status, seen as a climb-down from his former position as an Overseer in Grenada, stands in his way. He has an over-ambitious wife who plans and leads, often without referring to him. His experiences of racism, has reduced him to someone whose level of frustration causes him to just stay at home and play a guitar, go to the betting shop or hit his wife.

Joanne tells us that, ***"Life had been complicated, silent and pretentious and maybe best left alone to unravel its mysteries in the fullness of time,"* (p.295).** It is how Joanne has decided to deal with life's complication. Calvin's way of dealing with his situation was to opt out of the relationship, leaving his wife and children to survive on their own. There is a sense that patriarchy is emasculated since the men are unable to fulfill their expressed *destinies;* conversely, matriarchy could be seen as an overpowering force that also overshadows them.

Gran-gran's father

Gran-gran's father we learn had to struggle also, being left with 7 children to bring up after his wife, Gran-gran's mother, died; ***"Her father, who had been left to bring up their seven children, had spent his waking hours, solely occupied with making sure that they had enough food to eat and a roof over their heads, whilst the older girls***

***helped, where possible, to look after the younger ones. Their jobs were to support their father and to ensure that the general running of the house was smooth,"* (p.206)**. The dominant image of the male here is as a provider, with little time for anything else. Additionally, Gran-gran's children, Meena and Mary, also do not speak of their father except when Irene mentions in a letter, that her **"*family shame*" (p.168)** could have caused his death. The women are happily bringing up children and "fathering" them as they grow.

Randolph

In ***A Woman of Destiny,*** the **subject of the narrator's quest is to find Randolph, her absent father.** This calls into question the role of fathers and the image of fatherhood in the novel as a whole. Unlike Justin's dad, who was forced to marry Jessica and live a miserable, frustrated life, we are presented with Randolph's parents who demonstrate an over-protective role; bent on preventing their son from a fate similar to Justin's dad.

Randolph's absence as a father from Joanne's life is carefully orchestrated in two ways; dominated by his parents' judgment that he should not be tied down at an early age, Randolph disowns his unborn child to please them. It is also done in order to ensure that Randolph would have the kind of ***destiny*** they have projected for him. In their case, there is a strong need to project ***destiny*** as an overriding ambition for him; one which must not acknowledge his bastard child. Here, the sense and meaning of ***destiny*** for Randolph's parents, takes precedence over everything; so they make him reject his unborn child. For them, ***destiny*** is an ideal which must be hotly pursued, even when it means obliterating whatever stands in your way of claiming it. The second reason for the absence of the father in Joanne's life is also carefully orchestrated by Irene, to spite Randolph for his initial rejection.

Tony

Other men in ***A Woman of Destiny*** include **Tony, one of the twins' boyfriends in England. We see Tony via Irene's reaction to him** and this demonstrates the impact of negative life experiences Joanne's mum suffered. She firstly experienced a catastrophic relationship, which saw her demise, at her tender age of 15 years; the result of an 'unwanted' pregnancy and the shame that this brought on her family. She carries the "burden" that this may have killed her father. Additionally, Irene experienced difficulties with Calvin, who, to all intents and purposes, abandoned them; leaving her to bring up 3 girls on her own. Therefore, she uses her experiences to judge others and as a result, expresses grave concerns even **"*paranoia*"** about Darris' relationship with Tony.

To Irene, Tony is presented as someone who's not rooted; (having a past with a dead mother), and there is no mention of a father; Irene questions his morals and motives about his relationship with her daughter because he lives in government-assisted accommodation and wants to live with Darris before marriage; an idea that is abhorrent to Irene. She believes that these qualities do not readily make him eligible as a future partner for her daughter, especially as he did not seem to be doing things **"*the proper way,"* (p.292).** This situation was compounded by Irene's underlying motive – to show Calvin, the children's estranged father, **"*how well she had done without his help in***

bringing up her girls,"*(p293).** Like Randolph's parents, Tony did not meet the standards required for Irene's projected ***destiny for Darris. However, we commiserate with Irene's reasoning, that ***"Only those, whose backside is in the fire, know how hot it is!"*(p.292)**

The fall-out from such situations, where a person's ***destiny*** is being manipulated by others, where role-models appear to present a portrait of loneliness and despair, pessimism, with abortive dreams; present a risk of cultural splintering and downgrading the importance of personal choice in one's life.

Peter, Aunt Mary's son, who was born in England, has never been to the Caribbean landscape; limiting the majority of his interaction with the folk and folk tradition to only his mum, Aunt Mary in his household and Irene. He is impatient with cultural allegiance, and instead projects the, ***"the new generation's modern ideas and the fact that parents needed to understand that England was different from Grenada,"* (p.291).** Peter's future goal and solution to the problems of ineffective family relationships will be ***"to choose a white partner,"* (p.291).** The narrator surmises that this would present greater challenges, as there would be a wider scale of problems to deal with that includes ***"prejudices and discrimination"* (p.291)** resulting from a ***"mixed marriage,"* (p.291).**

The 'African Priest'

The 'African priest' represents deception in order to achieve his *destiny*. He resorts to corruption as an approach to achieving his ambitions and as a charlatan, took advantage of the vulnerability of the villagers. As someone who travelled frequently and whose finger was probably on the cultural and political pulse of the region, he picked up snippets of information in Trinidad to hatch his plan. A former trader between the islands, he understood the cultural vacuum that the fading colonisation was creating in the villagers' psyche and their need for a replacement of something new, from a different perspective.

Such a perspective, he surmised, would bridge the cultural and historical divide; especially **the attractiveness of the American Black Power Movement of the late 60's and early 70's.** It is for this reason he chose to come as an "African priest." The expressed ***"back to Africa"*** sentiments of the Movement, were not necessarily going back to Africa physically but represented **an aesthetic shift back to African culture, language, religion, and history; since Africa was being projected as the "*Motherland*" instead of England.**

The idea is that many saw raising black consciousness as the antidote for the 'damage' done by the longevity of colonisation on the psyche of the people of the region. Therefore, many were quick to embrace this idea of elevating 'blackness' as an inspirational strand for the approaching 'independence' of the island and a way forward.

Brother Charlie agreed that ***"the children must learn about their roots,"* (p.78)** when he enthusiastically endorsed and accepted the "*African Priest*" among the innocent children. It is because the dominance of such sentiments, no one in the village had questioned the priest's background. Therefore, he was given carte blanche and full discretionary powers to inadvertently 'abuse' the girls; right under the noses of their parents and Carers. It is for this reason the women were sorely disappointed that he escaped their revenge. Failing to attack him physically, and enraged that they were not able to confront him, they chose the next best thing to destroy him; pronouncing curses on his life, in Grenadian French Creole language. ***"That wretch! Pli maliwells! She continued cursing him in patwa, then warned, He better don' let me start on him wid me goat-mouth, noh! You know Goat-mouth bring poison prophecy!"* (p.114)**

At the outset, the narrator presented his appearance with scepticism as, ***"a Jewish Rabbi with a long bushy beard and black, tightly curled hair, hiding his face,"* (p.82).** The description also suggested his predatory attitude because ***"His quick, sharp eyes flashed around the room with interest; pleasantly surveying the young children as they walked one by one into the church,"* (p.82).** The pathetic imagery that follows is one where, despite the children's ***"protective parents accompanied them all,"* (p.106)** his greater plan deluded them, so that he had the last laugh. It was after this incident that Aunt Meena took matters in her own hands to announce a break with tradition in how adults in society are treated. We see her like a Major General, instructing the children as to what aspects of the cultural tradition they now take on board; fearing that their naivety had exposed them to grave danger.

This scenario is reflective of the political fights between superpowers - firstly France (1649-1763) and then England, (1763-1974); when the island was colonised and the people were subjugated by others for a period of 325 years. There is a suggestion that the fight continues but on other levels in society, therefore *vigilance* is being suggested as the watchword. Historically, the subsequent action by USA in 1983 by President Reagan, and the reasons given confirm the narrator's subtle views.

Manny

Manny, like Calvin, has a destiny that appears to be curtailled by circumstances in his domestic life. He has expressed ambitions of marrying Velma and buying a house in England but his past appears to catch up with him and therefore stands in the way of his progress. There is a sense here that a person's ambition/destiny can be affected by other people's manipulation. Manny is seen as a tragic figure with abortive dreams, whose happiness was short-lived due to Claudine's intervention.

Plot & Structure

Thompson's story is told by her narrator, Joanne, in two parts with different lengths. The subtitle directs how we view the structure of the book because it is described as *"A Calypso Novel."* This means that as a *"Calypso Novel,"* there is a suggestion that a **fusion of two genres** (the ***Calypso/song*** or ***oral narrative*** and the ***written text***); exist within this book. The reason for this perspective is that the book or ***written text*** presents the ***narrated stories as Calypsos***, regarded as ***oral*** genre. In other words, we should relate to this fusion because the ***narrated/spoken*** stories are also written down to create the ***literary text*****,** and together they resemble the ***oral characteristics of Calypsos*** in general.

The first section, **Part I**, is located in Grenada and **Part II** is located in England. **Part I** is longer and acts as a dramatic frame around the story – it contains a **Prologue**, with an opening tag that suggests the storytelling has begun. Rather like ***"crick crack"*** of the folks' storytelling tradition; we are presented with ***"As it was in the beginning***…in the **Prologue**, when the ***story/begins***, and later at the end of **Part II**, the ***conductor/narrator***, signals ***the end*** of the ***song/story*** with **… *"so shall it be in the end,"*** which prefaces the **Epilogue**.

Part I is the background where Joanne grows up and symbolically there is a sense that **her Calypso** is being created as she grows; with the support of the **folks' musical input backing her**. Joanne's **mother's *solo***, when she baths the child for the last time says, ***"You must listen"; "Learn your work good"; "Remember you must have a destiny," (p.38)*****.** These instructions suggest that Joanne will be able to ***write her story or sing her narration*** by first ***listening*** to her elders in the community, and ***learning*** by doing or acquiring knowledge; then ***remembering*** what she has been taught, (memory must always be actively engaged), so that she can transpose these qualities anywhere, in becoming that *Woman of Destiny* she is expected to be.

Therefore, her **narration/song** initially is one of **group-effort** to begin with, as it receives assistance and gradually takes shape with the help of other **narratives/songs**, as **solos**, **duo, trios, quartets**, and **group percussionists** in Grenada. Then, with these skills fully employed, Joanne is able to partially complete the majority of her **song/text** in the cultural and traditional environment. Afterwards, Joanne will take these qualities to far off territories, when she leaves Grenada, to continue her **song/narration** in England. There, she will apply all the rules and techniques, she has learnt earlier, as she extends and expands her creativity.

In *A Woman of Destiny*, Joanne's craft is cyclical; her **song/story** begins at the end, goes full circle then back to the end again. Joanne presents us with the content of her **story/song** in a **flashback**, so that we are given an insight into how her **text/song** was created, in the first place. As a trainee, Joanne is apprenticed by experienced villagers, as her **backing singers**. Their role is to add to her main narration, help in crafting her narrative and advise on pitfalls, as they guide her to where the best advantages could be gained, in **perfecting her song/narration**. Therefore, the ***villagers or backers*** come in with ***call-and-response techniques***; as is demonstrated with Joanne's tête-à-têtes with Gran-gran, Aunt Meena, Emma and her village friends, Reverend Blackman, and Justin's dad. In addition, there is also a variety of input consisting of **duo, trio, quartet or a whole group**. This is confirmed in Joanne's farewell event, Mark's funeral, and times with the 'African' priest in church; as well as occasions with groups of village children, throughout **Part I** of the novel.

However, in **Part II** Joanne struggles at being a ***soloist*** in the new environment; without much variety and the profusion of input we saw in **Part I**. Consequently, she has an outburst (**Chapter 9**), because of her contrasting experience, which she regards as ***"damn sameness"*** or ***"damn stupidness"* (p.238).** Joanne has learnt that in her new environment, her narration lacks vitality and she tells us, ***"I longed for difference – small and large brick house and wooden house, sapodilla, breadfruit, golden apple, governor-plum, mango, paw-paw, hog-plum, cushu and genip! Yes, even rivers and ravines, ponds and lakes, and big, wide, open spaces. Difference was everywhere in Grenada,"* (p.238).** Joanne's realizes the important part the Grenadian landscape played in her creative ***text/song*** and here her desperation for the landscape suggests her longing for the Grenadian folks/her ***backing band.***

The ***tone*** of Joanne's narration changes in **Part II**. The shift in focus is the different kind of input Joanne gets from migrant folks; whose ***songs/texts*** have also undergone major changes in ***tone*** and ***tempo.*** Therefore, there is difficulty in sustaining the ***rhythm*** and ***beat*** that she began with. In the **Epilogue**, Joanne returns to the environment for the finale; for a kind of final input from the folks. However, on her return she discovers that the general ***tone*** and ***rhythm*** of the ***song/narration*** in the old environment has changed too.

In addition, her ***song/narration*** now has a fusion of elements which have been added to from the foreign environment she has returned from. It means that the **original text** she began with is considerably **improvised and expanded**. There is a sense that Joanne returns not for approval, but to perform a duty; that of 'returning.' She will later go off to **sing her song,** and create her own narration as she sees fit. Her **new text** will embody aspects of the folk tradition but inevitably, there will be **improvisation** that will have become relevant to her 'new'/different environments. That being the case, there is a sense that inevitably, Joanne's **song/text** with its fused elements will be a **new creation** of her original **narration/song**.

Sub-Plots

The main plot in *A Woman of Destiny* is about Joanne, her immediate family in Grenada and later in England, as well as the complex relationship between both families. This leads to Joanne being left in Grenada to be cared for by her grandmother and aunt, when her mother migrates to England. Joanne subsequently migrates, some 9 years later, when she leaves Grenada to join a 'new' family in England. Calvin, her step-father in the 'new' family, later abandons the mother, leaving her to cope with Joanne and twin girls. Despite migrating to join her mother, the 13 year old Joanne has an underlying mission; which is to find her absent father based on the little information she has. She later discovers that there would have been no need for a personal quest, had she been told the truth about her past. She aborts her quest when the jig-saw puzzle of her life is fully fitted together, and when she understands the web of deceit her mother had spun before she died. She later returns to Grenada, to fulfill her mother's dying request to be buried in Grenada.

However, from this main story line, several smaller stories or subplots are hung. They're closely related to the main narrative but can be seen as separate stories that can be independent of the main plot.

The Subplots in *A Woman of Destiny* are:

- **Irene and Randolph's story** – a story of young love, teenage pregnancy, family dominance, hatred and death.

- **Aunt Meena** – a story of a family charged with the task of taking care of her sister's daughter, while the mother migrates; without a sense of a limit on the period of time the help is required for. Aunt Meena's insecurities/fears, the paranoia linked to her responsibility, and the extra single-handed task of looking after her ageing mother, Joanne's grandmother.

- **Aunty Mary** – the story of a migrant family in England, expectations, complicated realities and coping strategies.

- **The role of the outsider in Grenada** - Mr. Jessup and colonization in Grenada, Canadian missionaries and the 'African priest'.

The subplots help to reveal more about the main plot; they strengthen the themes within the main narrative, and deepen our insights into the lives of the main characters.

Style - Viewpoint

The story in ***A Woman of Destiny*** is told entirely by Joanne. She is an integral part of the events and situations she describes. She narrates the novel predominantly in a flashback style. For the most part, she presents information via the **"I"** persona, with other personal pronouns that shows inclusiveness of the folks, **"we", "us", "our"** within her first person narration. The first person narratives allow us to see and hear the things that Joanne sees, does and hears; about the people in her immediate circle and those she is linked with in some way.

However, the Author uses another style to allow other characters; such as Gran-gran, Aunt Meena, Justin's dad, Emma, and the village children, to **talk directly to Joanne** about things she does not do, neither see nor hear. We witness this when Gran-gran tells

Joanne about her life, her father and about Mr. McDonald; the person who raped her. We learn about **Hurricane Janet** from Aunt Meena and Gran-gran; Justin provides information about the 'African priest', and Justin's dad, gives us an insight into the style of colonial education he and his contemporaries received. **Irene's letters from England** provide information about the migrants' struggles and personal problems they face in England. **Joanne learns things she has not personally experienced from her best friend** Emma, who is allowed a greater degree of freedom than Joanne is; so she fills her in about carnival celebrations, which Joanne is banned from attending.

Another narrative technique is used to allow Joanne to **overhear information from adults' conversation**, that are not really meant for her to hear – Gran-gran and Miss Joseph's gossip on the verandah, about a young village girl's pregnancy and the ensuing dilemma; listening to the villagers farewell after she is put to bed by her mother; Aunt Meena and Miss Cleothilda's conversation in La Bay about Christopher and his mother's predicament in England; hearing information from the village girls about England in St. John's river; overhearing Calvin slapping and then having a scuffle with Irene.

As a young 10 year old in Grenada, she narrates the cultural tradition and her language shows her subservient personality; she answers questions with one word answers ***"yes,"*** and does not elaborate much on conversations. Even with Gran-gran she plays more of a **"listener"** than **"a talker" (p.52);** since she is supposed to be ***"seen and not heard,"*** **(p.16)** lest she becomes guilty of ***"asking too many questions,"*** **(p.16).** However, as she grows, Joanne becomes more assertive and we see this firstly via her interactions with Emma, Justin and her village friends.

Later, Joanne's tone changes as she grows up in England and we hear her views, as she describes her initial reaction to England; details of a holiday fiasco to the West Country, in England, and when she takes charge of her mother's welfare, prior to her death. Her maturity of tone is seen in the assessment she later makes of her situation; ***"But adults, I had decided many years ago, were perfect at playing the game of "Hate-Till –Death,"*** **(p.294).**

At this point, Joanne has developed an adult way of viewing things and uses her experiences to make judgments and decisions because, ***"time had tempered the many years of wishful thinking. Instead, it had schooled me, in the realities of what is seen and experienced,"*** **(p.294).** This mature tone and way of reasoning is now the grown-up Joanne; who can now talk as an adult, ***"Life had been complicated, silent and pretentious and maybe best left alone to unravel its mysteries in the fullness of time,"*** **(p.294).** Ultimately, she is commentator on the behaviour of others in the novel and the wider situation in Grenada and England.

Style - **Setting and Atmosphere**

The action in *A Woman of Destiny* takes place in two settings - Grenada and England. **Part I** is in a village, in the Parish of St. Andrews, Grenada, where Joanne's home is located. This area is in the North West of the island, which has a small airport. Joanne walks 3 miles to a location where she takes the bus to her secondary school in Grenville, the island's second town. Aunt Meena sells her land produce in a market in La Bay; a seafront in Grenville.

In establishing a strong sense of place, every aspect of our senses is engaged when the narrator describes the landscape. She presents the village as something that's not only physical, but one which soothes, gives comfort, hope, peace, forgiveness and restores. ***"As I stood there the beauty of the place punctuated my thoughts with flashes of our childhood exploits and the glory of those days,"* (p.2).** Later, she tells us ***"I took in deep, fresh, breaths of air, soaking in this spiritual renewal and my mind became sanguine once more,"* (p.2).**

Therefore, the landscape has a number of impacting qualities on a person's whole being; emotional and physical; cultural and spiritual. ***"I drew fresh courage from the quietness of the place,"* (p.4).** Later, we are invited to engage our feelings and we feel the breeze as she narrates, ***"the rustling leaves in the gentle breeze soothed my spirit and whispered the need for comfort and hope, peace and forgiveness,"* (p.4).** However, that same landscape is also steeped in cultural beliefs where, ***"many had already feared the tree's association with death, evil and the belief that there, lost souls who are unable to rest in peace, roamed the land of the living,"* (p.3)** became ***"the silk cotton tree was a symbol of witchcraft. Obeah men, we were told on storytelling nights, could catch a person's soul and nail it on a silk cotton tree,"* (p.3).**

The descriptive language used to portray the setting and atmosphere, is meant to deliberately communicate the landscape in highly visual, imagistic and regenerative terms. We see this each time the locality is described, down to the minutest details, of how the houses are arranged; the Junction and its environs; the activities of mad ants; the reminiscent downpour; or women washing clothes in St. John's river; give an atmosphere that is enhanced by Thompson's descriptions.

In highly atmospheric writing, Joanne describes what she sees in the locality around her, and we learn about the uses she puts to the local flora and herbs, e.g. the benefits of ***"careila* bush** and ***bois den* spice leaf,** with some ***black sage,*** when she makes a homeopathic bath for Gran-gran; ***"my job was to rub in the herbally-infused medicine which I learnt was good for pain, rheumatism, colds, soothing hurt emotions, and loving her,"* (p.16).** Traditional wisdom is passed on to Joanne by Gran-gran who educates her on the benefits of the landscape to the folks; ***"Careila cleanses the blood," she had told me one day. "That bitter-bush is good for your inside and outside too,"* (p.21).**

That the landscape has healing qualities is uncontested, as the passengers on buses also discuss their individual benefits as they advise one another about what to use. Joanne tells us that Gran-gran ***"often coached me on the varieties and cures and I learned to recognise the natural herbal remedies by sight. The lemon grass which she tended behind the house was good for tea and slight fever,"* (p.22).**

Joanne also brings the atmosphere closer to us by making us smell and almost taste the local fish, when she describes Aunt Meena's cooking. ***"The aroma of cocoa-tea with cinnamon spice filled our house as Aunt Meena made the breakfast. She fried bakes and salt fish,"* (p.18).** After her day's market sale, she is busily preparing food that evokes the Grenadian setting. We learn about ***golden apples, governor plums, cushu, avocado pears*** and, **"some mango types - *Lung, Starchie and Grafted,"* (p.55).** From things to eat to what we seen, we are told about ***damsel tree, bougainvillea, hibiscus, and jump-up-and-kiss-me*** flowers; to what she watches, as the ***mad ants*** and ***fireflies*** that make the atmosphere unmistakably tropical.

However, the tropical weather can also present the dark side of nature; from its scary **Hurricane Janet,** as well as downpours that cause death and flooding, or rivers to overflow and burst their banks, to the sun's crematory heat. The idea is that nature can be paradise but the idyllic descriptions are not always what they seem. ***"The sun could be seen miles away over selected areas in the distance, where it had chosen to linger; before giving way to the threats of thunder and downpour in our village,"* (p.59).** Even Joanne is ***"mesmerized by the dominance of the water and how it had forced itself on everything in sight,"* (p.60).** Additionally, the potential for violence is ever-present in the rustic landscape; from beatings at home, at school or on the street; to murder.

Joanne and the girls in her family grow up in a restricted atmosphere. They are limited in the activities they attend and may be occasionally fortunate to accompany either Aunt Meena to the market in La Bay or the main town in St. Georges, where she is able to see "*big people.*" The girls are not allowed to take part in the annual carnival but the atmosphere of religious practices dominates their lives. Joanne's training for her destiny is tied up with her learning to read daily to her grandmother from her "*Words of Comfort,*" where the atmosphere is one of control and restriction.

Girls are not allowed to talk to boys, and do not know what to do when they have their menstrual cycle but are given cryptic advice without explanations; hence they must find their own ways to accumulate knowledge beyond the confines of their parents' dominance. Aunt Meena disproves of Joanne's friendship with Justin and there is a strict routine, (even when storytelling), which does not allow the children of the household any free time.

The atmosphere in Justin's dad's household, or certainly where boys are reared, is different and we are invited to compare the different styles of upbringing between boys and girls. Boys are allowed to come and go independently, imitate men-talk and roam freely. The children of the village are not well-informed and appear to puzzle out their existence by chatting while engaged in work e.g. washing clothes in the river. Hence, Joanne is forced to steal Aunt Meena's letters in order to learn about life.

In England, the atmosphere at home is strained and Joanne tells us that there were conflicts caused by arguments about money, violence and the eventual family breakup. There is an obvious difference in atmosphere between Joanne at home in Grenada and at Joanne at home in England. The vibrancy of the life of the folks is absent in England. The quietness and ***"sameness"*** which Joanne abhors, contrasts the colours and differences found in the Grenadian landscape. It leads Joanne to question and challenge the way of life she has led and vows to become more independent in her thinking, self-directed and selective of aspects of her culture that she takes on board.

Themes

A theme is either an idea or set of ideas that runs through a text (oral and literary). In the case of ***A Woman of Destiny,*** which has many themes, we see the various themes overlapping, as they weave in and out of sections, forming patterns to make the whole text.

In ***A Woman of Destiny***, there are several themes which could be considered as follows:

The novel's main themes are:

- Music
- Family
- Education
- Migration
- Storytelling
- Childhood & growing up
- Religion
- Matriarchy/motherhood
- Fatherhood
- Language
- Landscape - tradition & culture
- Empowerment/destiny

Lesser but related themes are:

- Tragedy
- Post-independence blues
- Belief systems
- Sexual Exploitation & corruption
- Gossip
- Violence
- Obeah

No theme in the novel is completely separate from others which make up the text. For example, we see the theme of childhood, when there is discussion about the family, religion, language, mother and fatherhood, education, and empowerment/destiny. In fact, the theme of childhood is interrelated to each one of the lesser themes in the novel. Similarly, discussions about the family highlight religious intolerance of aspects of culture, the role of colonization, landscape, migration, education and so on. The fact is, some themes feature more regularly than others as they form the pattern of the novel.

Music and the Significance of the Calypso

Lord Kitchener

The novel's subtitle suggests we should read the book as a **Calypso**. For those who don't know what a Calypso is they are invited to find out what it is. At the same time we are being asked to understand how it is applied in the novel to make it a "***Calypso text***," and what combining the two (**Calypso/song** and written **text/book**); adds to our understanding and appreciation of the novel.

The terms "***Calypso* and *Novel***" suggest that a **fusion of these two genres** (the Calypso or oral narrative and the written text); exist within this book. In other words, the book or ***written text*** presents the narrated stories as ***Calypsos,*** which are ***oral*** genres. This therefore produces a fusion so that although the story or narration is being told to us, it uses the written form to create the literary text.

This combination or fusion of forms in ***A Woman of Destiny,*** is an experimental approach that challenges the conventions of the Caribbean literary canon. By incorporating characteristics of the Calypso into the text in the way that it does, the novel is honouring all aspects of Caribbean forms of expression and this opens up new possibilities for the reader, when reading Caribbean literary narratives.

Chalkdust

What we have as a result, is a novel that can be improvisational and digressive, flashing backwards and forwards, teaming with the vibrancy of Caribbean life, as it presents the Grenadian folks in a landscape that can never be taken at face value. Therefore, tolerance is needed to understand the underlying, structural significance of the thematic approaches through the lens of Calypso music. This will help the reader to adapt him or herself to the expressive powers of the Calypso in the narrative and to appreciate the new possibilities that it presents for both Author and readers of the text.

The background to Calypso music is associated with carnival and carnivalesque forms of revelling and lifestyles. The word "*Calypso*" is said to have derived from several linguistic backgrounds; meaning a joyous song ***"carieto"***, or drinking party or festivity. Additionally, it is referred to in French (archaic) as ***carouse or carrouseaux***. During the process of Anglicization of the language in the Caribbean region, the word ***"caliso"*** was used; Spanish for a topical song. It is also referred to in West African, Hausa, as ***Kaiso;*** when used to express approval and encouragement, similar to **"bravo!"** in applause.

What is a Calypso?

A Calypso is a style of Caribbean music that originated from Trinidad and Tobago during the early 20th century. The original The original rhythm of the Calypso can be traced back to West Africa and the arrival of French Planters and their slaves from the region known as the *French Antilles* in the 1600s. The term *French Antilles* or French West Indies, (also known in French as: *Antilles françaises*), refers to the seven territories which are currently under French rule in the Caribbean area known as *Antilles*. Therefore Calypso, as a musical style, drew on African and French influences. The musical style was defined by its highly rhythmic and harmonic vocals and this was Sung in a French Creole Language, led by a *griot.*

Aaron Duncan

A g*riot*, similar to a travelling musician in West Africa, was a singer and storyteller who sung about the condition of society exactly as it was – hence the phrase, ***"telling it like it is."*** In Plantation days, slaves often used these songs to mock their slave-masters and they used the opportunity to communicate with each other about their plans to rebel.

The *griot* would sing praise or abuse in his repertoire and later was referred to as a ***chantuelle***. As the music developed and the language in Trinidad changed, the word ***Calypsonian*** was used to describe the person singing the Calypso song in a local Trinidadian language known as ***Trinidadian French Creole***. This is a mixture of French and Trinidadian English, called *Patois* (pronounced pat-wa). Later, when English became the dominant language in Trinidad, the Calypso was sung in English. This attracted attention from the government who realized that the songs had a powerful influence on the population, who listened to the lyrics intently. The information contained in the Calypsos allowed the masses to challenge political Authorities; in particular, an unelected Governor and Legislative Council in two town councils in Trinidad.

Consequently, Calypso became a kind of influential **'weapon,'** as it had the power to sway the masses and therefore played an important role in politics. Simultaneously, the songs were documenting the history of Trinidad and Tobago; in ways which made them a kind of ***"people's newspaper,"*** and the Calypsonian being the ***people's representative,*** was daubed the ***"people's mouthpiece."*** In so doing, both the Calypso and the Calypsonian became ***"the voice of the people."***

The main characteristic of the Calypso is ***communication***; the voice in communication with an audience, with or without the addition of percussion instruments. The performance can take the form of a person singing in the extempore genre i.e., composing on the spot. In the early days, the songs usually involved aggressive language, when Calypso contestants traded insults among one another in a performance called ***Mepris*** or a kind of ***"war of Calypsos"*** for the best executed Calypso. Such styles were full of satire, wit, and demonstrated competitive linguistic mastery.

Calypso Rose- "Calypso Queen of the World"

The Calypsonian's chosen nickname was significant in this battle of words, therefore combative titles which inspired fear in the opponent were chosen. Names such as ***Attila the Hun,*** was chosen for its linkages with being one of the most feared enemies of the Eastern and Western Roman Empires. ***Lord Melody***, for example, wished to indicate that he was the lord of melodious singing, while others chose community-based or childhood nick-names e.g. ***The Mighty Sparrow;*** which indicated something about their personalities or characters. All the Calypso extracts in ***A Woman of Destiny***, are composed by Calypsonians with similar impressive and combative titles.

In the ***"war of Calypsos"*** a performer would sing a verse and then his competitor is allowed to reply. He would do so by responding to the verse sung or by singing about his competitor. These may range from insults about his competitor's appearance, the clothes they are wearing to derogatory comments about physical attributes. This type of aggressive verbal word play was referred to as ***pekong*** or ***piquant*** (meaning, biting or stinging); where someone is allowed to insult another for fun.

Other styles of singing Calypso can vary with the voice ***telling it like it is;*** which means being as critical as they want to and making social and political commentary via either (recorded transmission or in communication with a live audience). Often the live audience would respond directly to the Calypsonian and this is called the ***call-and-response*** style. It can be a spontaneous verbal interaction between the singer and the listener, so that when the singer ***"calls"*** it is met with expressions or ***"responses"*** from the listener. This style of interaction has its background in African culture, where the ***call-and-response*** is a dominant pattern of participation in gatherings. In the Caribbean as in Africa, this style is used in meetings, religious rituals, children's rhymes and musical expressions e.g. also in America seen in blues, jazz, hip-hop and gospel music.

The ***call-and-response*** style of worship is demonstrated in ***A Woman of Destiny*** in the church service with Reverend Blackman and his congregation in **Chapter 3**. The Reverend Blackman prays and the congregation responds:

"We want to tank you Gawd for this country of ours Lawd."
"Yes!"
"For Ministers of the gospel."
***"Yes, Lawd!"* (p.85)**

Calypso is also associated with Carnival celebrations which have played an important role in developing Calypso music in Trinidad and Tobago. The music has transformed from African percussion, banned in 1881 to bamboo **(*tamboo-bamboo*),** sticks beaten together, which was also banned. In 1937, they were transformed as an orchestra of frying pans, dustbin lids and oil drums. However, the steel pan orchestras we know today, made up of ***pans or steel drums,*** are a major part of the Trinidadian music scene and steel band music is played in Primary and Secondary schools in Britain and around the world. The popularity of Calypsos has spread throughout the Caribbean and the world, having begun its milestone in 1914, the year of the first Calypso recording. It is an art-form that has been dominated by men until 1978 when a woman, ***Calypso Rose*** (Martha Linda Sandy-Lewis - whose career as a Calypsonian spans over 40 years), won the annual Calypso competition, so that the competition title was changed from ***"Calypso King Competition"*** to ***"Calypso Monarch Competition."*** Today the art-form has evolved and some of the changes reflect the cultural influences that make up of the Caribbean region.

Many of the varieties of Calypsos found in the Caribbean region, include genres that are characteristic of the original Calypso but with an individual style of separate island input. Around the Caribbean islands these forms are: ***Mento*** – a style of Jamaican folk music (which influenced ***ska*** and ***reggae***), and also in Jamaica, ***Ska***, which came before ***rocksteady*** and ***reggae.*** In Barbados it is reflected by ***Spouge,*** a popular Barbadian music. In Dominica, it is referred to as ***Cadence-lypso***, which is a mixture of Calypso with the ***cadence*** of Haiti. In Antigua and Barbuda, it's referred to as the ***Benna genre*** and a more modern form of the Calypso has evolved, known as *soca* music, which is a style of ***Kaiso/Calypso;*** with influences that demonstrate native blends. These are: ***cadence-lypso, chutney soca; with its East Indian influence, rapso,* and *ragga soca,*** as well as ***soul*** and ***funk*** music.

How the Calypso is applied in the Novel

This ***Calypso Novel,*** is set in the early 1970's, with a focus on a Grenadian village in the parish of St. Andrews - ***landscape***. It validates a sense of place, mood, and projects the vitality of characters that populate it, as essential to the plot of the Calypso tune – ***the audience.*** However, that Grenadian village is also symbolic and representative of any other Caribbean island village, which experienced aspects of the main themes in the novel – Caribbean extended families caring for children who have been left at home, whilst parents migrate to the metropolis – UK, USA, Canada or elsewhere; in order to seek betterment abroad and the resultant complexities experienced by all those involved.

The main characteristic of the Calypso is ***communication***. Communication, in the case of this novel, is realized by a ***narrator/composer***, in engagement with a *'**live audience**'*, or its readers. Whether with our without lyrics, episodes within the narrative are reminiscent of the musical genre as they ***'sing'*** the life of the people via performance, speech-making, folk and religious transmissions, ***ole talk***, storytelling, gossip or giving the ***lowdown***. Additionally, this is done through whatever varieties of the Grenadian vernacular is projected; ***Grenada Creole, French Creole or Patois*** (pronounced ***pat-wa***); or Standard English, as they are uttered among the different generations within the novel.

Singing Sandra

The most obvious allusion to the Calypso musical genre is the examples of 13 Calypsos presiding over each Chapter in the novel, as a way of honouring the past oral **master-Calypsonians** of the musical genre. These early Calypsonians are among those who have maintained a determination and insistence, through their repertoire, on giving respectability to the Calypso over the past 100 years, so that we can learn to appreciate it, with the current global significance it now enjoys.

A case in point is that Steel band music is taught in British and other European schools, as part of their curriculum, brings as never before, Calypso and pan music to the fore and widening its global frame of reference. The early Calypsos existed at a time when singing them was unpopular; when they were censured or banned because the **lyrics**, whether interpreted as negative or positive, were used to influence political thought and to sway the mass population into action. It can be seen that the Calypso lyrics embody subject matters that document the whole spectrum of life, as it is lived in all aspects of society; thereby giving the Calypsonian's repertoire an ***archival function*** within society.

In ***A Woman of Destiny***, the pioneering Calypsonians who appear at the beginning of each Chapter are some of the historical giants of the Calypso tradition, who helped to perpetuate this art form over the past 100 years. Names such as ***Attila the Hun*** (Raymond Quevado), ***Lord Invader*** (Rupert Grant) and ***Lady Iere*** (Edna Pierre), stood out, but there were many others who made an unforgettable contribution to Calypso music: ***Lord Kitchener*** (Aldwin Roberts) and ***The Mighty Sparrow*** (Dr. Francisco Slinger), are among the most prolific bards ever. ***Lord Caresser*** *(*Rufus Callendar), ***Lord Beginner*** (Egbert Moore), ***Lord Executor*** (Phillip Garcia), ***The Mighty Terror*** (Fitzgerald Henry) and ***Lord Shorty*** (Hollis Liverpool) have inspired generations with their creative artistry.

Their subject matters and style of content of Calypsos are unlimited and all aspects of society are "***written***" in the songs, include: humour, politics, sex, love, cricket, freedom, prostitution, witchcraft, marriage deceit, migration, government impropriety, social changes in society, the changing Calypso, partying, fêting, bacchanal, political and social commentary at home and abroad, gossip e.g. a man in the Queen's bedroom and numerous world news events are inscribed in the Calypso.

Symbolically, and in the tradition of cultural respect for Elders, in order to sing her own Calypso, Joanne is aided or is given a ***rite de passage*** by her elder presiding Calypsonians, to ***'sing'*** through her ***dilemma/song***, as they themselves have done in the past and continue to do today. Therefore, the Calypso at the beginning of each Chapter functions as an acknowledgement in the text, with messages that suggest meaning within the Chapter content as follows:

Chapter 1	We learn instructively of "**a mother's duty"**
Chapter 2	We are educated on the **characteristics of the Calypso**; "bewitching" "fascinating", "throbbing, "absorbing" Calypso rhythm.
Chapter 3	Presents a **warning to Mothers** on bringing up their daughters
Chapter 4	Sings a **caution** on the need for solidarity and love for one another
Chapter 5	Sings of the dilemma of Caribbean migrants in London
Chapter 6	**Inspires determination** and **allegiance** to Britain as the motherland
Chapter 7	Presents **inequality** in society
Chapter 8	Takes you back to the **occult religious forms** of obeah or witchcraft, being practiced in the region.
Chapter 9	**Advocates love for fathers**, regardless of their shortcomings.
Chapter 10	**Speaks politically**; tongue-in-cheek via parables, about **what voters' actions should be**, regarding the **inefficiency and ineffectiveness of those in power**.
Chapter 11	Personalises the **effects of colonial history** on the region;
Chapter 12	**Informs the populace** about the **vagaries of migration** for those who've left the Caribbean and
Chapter 13	**Presents regret**, in **a kind of diasporic 'blues'**, for those who have left the Caribbean to settle in London.

So like a Calypsonian, the narrator in ***A Woman of Destiny: A Calypso Novel***, tells us like is; by becoming ***"the people's/readers' newspaper"*** or ***"mouthpiece;"*** documenting all aspects of her landscape/society in her **story/Calypso**, throughout the novel. Her subject matter embodies the following, though not limited to these main events.

- The fight between Jean and Dessima
- Gospelypso:(an off-shoot of the Calypso) in the village church services
- Sukram's murder and the ensuing drama
- Mark's death – a village in mourning
- Verna, Christopher and the fiasco in England
- The dilemmas of immigrant Grenadians in Britain
- The *Man-of-words* at the narrator's Farewell
- Grenada's Independence
- The sapodilla incident and the English Headmaster's corporal punishment
- The village children's innocent discussions based on hear-say

- The Corrupt "*African priest*" - castor oil purge and the women's curses
- The Funeral of the Caribbean/Grenadian returnee
- The mother's experiences at work in England
- Gossiping and family dilemmas about pregnant unwed daughters
- The holiday experiences of the youth in England
- The Queen and the Duke's visit to the Caribbean region
- The fathers who don't look after their children and the mothers who 'father' them

There are numerous digressions, tangents and flashbacks as the narrative weaves back and forth between late 1960's and early 1970's, with a densely populated collection of characters in the two different landscapes **(Grenada and London)**. These present an idiosyncratic narrative structure of the novel that alludes to the influence that the genre of Calypso music had on the narrator. Her lack of participation in carnival festivities intensified her interest in it and made her acutely aware of its traditional value and implications, despite being instructed to the contrary.

Joanne tells us that despite her family's rejection of this aspect of Grenadian culture, her interest in the Calypso/carnival intensified. It confirms the power of the Calypso to influence thoughts and actions; especially since rejection of the popular Calypso lyrics had pertained to a priest taking part in carnival one year. The lyrics which suggests breaking all religious boundaries and joining in the bacchanal, gave licence to the listener to do likewise, ***"If the priest could play who is we?"* (p.54).** According to her family, this was somehow blasphemous. Therefore, as children, they were banned from showing an open interest in or taking part in the yearly carnival festivities. Conversely, this brought her closer to the island's tradition, and in this context, Calypso music can be seen to disrupt lives or present a challenge to the status quo.

Likewise, in the context of this novel, Calypso music disrupts the reader's conventional approach to the literary text. As with Calypso music, the narrative structure of ***A Woman of Destiny: A Calypso Novel*** disrupts expectations that the reader has developed while reading conventionally written texts. The difference in the book's narrative structure, calls for a distinct reading strategy, where the musical framework is the inter-textuality of the text. So too must the reader of this novel take his or her cue from the Calypso musical genre, in order to understand the most effective ways of evaluating the text.

Joanne's story is her Calypso being composed, and includes the essence of the whole 13 Calypsos enshrined at the beginning of each Chapter. They exemplify a Calypso composition in the making – beginning with a ***solo composition***, when she introduces both the **Prologue** and **Epilogue**. As a master Calypsonian herself, her dialogue/story is her art-form. In her ***backing musical band***, many Calypsonians are given a hearing, as in a ***Calypso competition***. Some ***speechify*** (as in Joanne's farewell event), demonstrate the competitive and ***linguistic mastery*** i.e. word play, pun, oration, humour, satire, double entendre – characteristic elements of the old Calypsonians.

The church congregation, at the beginning of the novel, projects the *call-and-response*, structure of the Calypso, evidenced by Reverend Blackman's prayer in the church service. Within the novel as a whole, the *bass percussion instruments* are provided by the men who are hardly audible, mainly around the rum shop; with *bass solos* playing in and out of Joanne's *medley* to either *praise or abuse*. These are mixed in with the *alto and soprano percussion* of the mothers in the *Calypso band.* They are very vocal, loud, sometimes playing as *solos, duos* (Irene and Gran-gran; Gran-gran and Miss Mattis, Cleothilda and Irene or as a *whole syncopation,* as provided by the initial introduction of a *two-piece band/duo percussionist* provided by Dessima and Jean in the fight. In their *mêlée*, they were joined by *bass instruments* (men's intervention) and added to by a *whole band;* the men and women who intervene and stop the fight. The *bacchanal* the fight produces is carnivalesque, reminiscent of the *Calypso performance* in *carnival.*

Whereas the creativity of Joanne's Calypso is most demonstrative of *group* creativity in its making, seen in **Part I** of the novel; **Part II** evidences a return to *solo* creativity in an unknown territory or landscape (England). Joanne has to almost re-create her narrative, as she treads through unknown territory. There the *solo* pieces/stories present a quieter *rhythm*, with a *slower pace;* returning to the *solo lyrics* or the voice in engagement with the main narrative/Calypso. All the other competitive elements, we saw in **Part I**, the support of the *band/family* and landscape in her formative years, have given way to a *single voice* in the main **narrative/composition**, and we regain focus by listening, via the reading, to why the whole *composition/story* began in the first place.

Joanne's composition began as a *solo 'as it was in the beginning'* and just as with all the difficulties and struggles the Calypso encountered to survive, Joanne's determination, staying-power, and insistence on form, structure and content, is what she has learnt, will see her through *'to the end'*. Born out of a bitter-sweet beginning in the Caribbean, she must learn to manipulate both elements, guided by those who were part of her beginning (Gran-gran and Irene, *her master Calypsonians*), to *'end'* with her own *composition* as she sees fit.

Therefore, *Joanne's solo*, as it was in the beginning, suggests that the characteristics of the forerunners of today's Calypso, still exist and therefore it will continue to every narrator/Calypsonian's 'end'. However, the idea of an *'end'* here is elusive. It suggests having several possibilities by its open-endedness and can be analysed according to what one makes of her *Calypso composition/her narrative*. With such exemplary characteristics forged by the making of the Calypso, it is possible to see how the novel title – *A Woman of Destiny*, will be realized in Joanne, as someone who has learnt the art from her *Calypso masters (griots)*, to make her villagers' prediction; becoming a *woman of destiny*, highly probable. This would be achievable whether she encounters, *censorship, ban, praise and abuse,* or *approval;* she becomes a ***griot*****,** a mistress Calypsonian, using her *song/story* to *"tell it like it is"* then she *fades* out on a certain note, with a question, as the *music trails off.*

Family Relationship

The two families at the heart of *A Woman of Destiny* consist of:

(1). **In Grenada** they family are: Gran-gran, Aunt Meena, Aunt Irene (migrated to England), Joanne's cousins - Ann, Monica, Yvonne, Lydia (Aunt Meena's children) and Joanne.

(2). **In England** the extended family are: Calvin (Stepfather), Aunt Mary, Peter (her son), Joanne's sisters, Darris & Dareen (twins); her mother Aunt Irene and Joanne, (now migrated to England).

The Family in Grenada

In the family in Grenada, Thompson shows us their life together more than in **Part II** or with any other family mentioned because Joanne, the narrator, has first-hand experience of the relationship between them so she uses the **"I"** perspective. We are told about others in the novel; such as Justin and his dad, Emma and Phyllis, and Emery and his uncle in the Great House, by what she observes or hears about them. The novel focuses on the relationship among the ***trio***, Gran-gran, Aunt Meena and Joanne and shows the different styles of upbringing and function of the adults.

Gran-Gran

Gran-gran is patient, long-suffering (having lost a son in England over dubious circumstances and separated from her daughters - Aunt Irene and Mary in England); is respected, encourages, teaches or instructs, rarely bantering or laughing but plays the role of the superior matriarch in the family. Traditionally, she is the head, who transmits traditional wisdom; is referred to over disputes or conflicts among her family; her decisions are respected and treated as final, and she commands the respect as an elder from different perspectives.

She is a senior mother in the church ***(religious level),*** is effectively the head of the home ***(traditional/cultural level),*** is shown respect by members of the villagers, hence her name given as a term of endearment ***"Gran-gran",*** among the children of the village; (cultural level). We are told **that *"Mothers who were the most senior or the church elders. They were the passers of wisdom, tradition and discipline. Seniority was revered and greatly accepted by all," (Cultural tradition)* (p.87).**

Thompson projects the relationship between Joanne and Gran-gran as an image of peace, as she constantly seeks peace and quietude from her ***"Words of Comfort".*** Her manner exudes peacefulness and this enables her to be tolerant of the two generations of family she has witnessed; across two different political eras; (ending of French domination and beginning of British domination of Grenada). As a result, her character bridges the language gap, so that she is able to use **French Creole** and **English Creole** to her great advantage.

Aunt Meena

We learn about the loving relationship between Joanne and her grandmother, and the dictatorial Aunt Meena. A strict disciplinarian, she has 4 girls of her own – Ann, Monica, Yvonne, Lydia and also takes care of Joanne, her sister Irene's daughter. Aunt Meena was a shrewd business woman, who sold provisions at the market in La Bay. She **"*laughed bellyfuls*" (p.111),** had an uncanny habit of being serious and laughing, at the same time.

She was quick to punish the girls, seemed fearful in her role as Caretaker of her sister's child; in case ***"anything should go wrong,"* (p.52).** With Aunt Meena, the atmosphere is always tense, rarely did she relax, and quite vigilant over the girls so that she rules with an iron fist. As a result, when she discovered that things had gone amiss during her **"watch,"** she was deeply disturbed and felt usurped by the 'African priest' who had got away with his misdemeanours.

The only time Aunt Meena seemed relaxed and jovial was during the Hurricane Janet story. She respectfully took her turn and showed respect for seniority when she and Gran-gran shared sections of the **Hurricane Janet** story being told to the village children. We know very little about Aunt Meena as there is no talk of a husband. She is unable to offer Joanne more information about the history of the country other than to confirm that **"*brave West Indian men, going to fight for England,*" (p.71).** However, she is quick to shut others out, when they probe, with her cryptic language and favourite catch-phrase, "***you ask too much questions"* (p.16)** or that ***"children must be seen and not heard,"* (p.16).**

Thompson projects Aunt Meena's character with a slight contrast from Gran-gran's because the women each have a different task to perform with Joanne. Both women are extremely vigilant over the girls and we see this when Aunt Meena follows the girls late one evening to the Junction, (**Chapter 1**); when she sees them misbehaving, she beats them with a stick. Gran-gran also uses her experience when she perceived Joanne's unhappiness with the 'African priest', and was able to deal with the situation in a vastly different way from Aunt Meena. It is noteworthy that after this incident, Aunt Meena took matters into her own hands to announce a break with tradition. We see her like a Major General, instructing the children as to what aspects of the cultural tradition they should now take on board, fearing that their naivety had exposed them to grave danger. In other words, culture and tradition need to be altered in order to give way and accommodate changes in society, when it's deemed necessary.

Joanne

Joanne is the narrator of the story in the novel. She was left by her mother, Irene, at the age of 10, when Irene migrated to England; leaving Joanne in the care of her Aunt Meena and Gran-gran, her grandmother. She meekly obeys her grandmother and Aunt Meena in everything. Joanne is conditional to an extreme form of Baptist religion, and is made to read daily passages in Gran-gran's *Words of Comfort*. The family's brand of religion does not acknowledge Carnival as a cultural tradition, and Joanne is prevented from involvement in its festivities, by being told ***"it's the work of the devil,"* (p.54).** Joanne is deeply troubled by her reality of not having a father, and with a mother who is hell-bent on keeping her in the dark about the details. Consequently, she feels she must investigate her past in order to make sense of the present.

Joanne learns ***by doing***, and is apprenticed by Gran-gran and Aunt Meena who both teach her. Within their family, physical punishment is a reality and this keeps Joanne and her cousins; Ann, Monica, Yvonne and Lydia, in check. She learns about the outside world (beyond her home, church and school), from her best friend Emma, who she is very attached to. In the novel, Joanne is singled out among the girls she is surrounded by, to be a ***Woman of Destiny***. Therefore, a lot is invested in her future, in terms of what being a ***Woman of Destiny*** mean to the old folks.

Her character is one of determination, as she overcomes various events that threaten to break her spirit; the incident with Justin's dad when he puts her down, ***"you could never pass an exam,"* (p.77).** Joanne nurses her hurt emotion but is able to come back with a resounding defiant statement; ***"I will be somebody, I will be a woman of destiny,"* (p.81).** She pursues this vision passionately, and we learn much about her characteristics from the definition of what being a ***Woman of Destiny*** really means to her mother, Reverend Blackman, (the priest of their church); Gran-gran, the villagers and to herself. Thompson presents Joanne as an ambitious, studious, and obedient 10 year old; who unquestionably, follows the rules as a loving grand-daughter and niece.

As an adolescent who is developing normal adult feelings and urges, she is desperate to learn about tabooed subjects such as having her menstrual cycle; the consequences of talking to boys and what to do when they make advances. Joanne, like the other girls in the village, tends to puzzle out these natural occurrences by themselves, and is reliant on hearsay, personal experiences and gossip. Joanne and the girls in their church are victims of the ***"big stick"*** which is Aunt Meena's rod of punishment; sexual advances from the ***"African priest;"*** and a very emotive, graphic form of corporal punishment that was publicly witnessed by 500 children in school; what in the 21st century would be regarded as ***"child abuse."***

There is a gulf between Joanne and her mother, and we see this as the underlying reasons for this distance, in the details of the mother's past relationship with Randolph, Joanne's father. Her mother does not have any of the little confidential conversations with Joanne, as we witness between Joanne and her grandmother in **Part I.** There is also very little motivation shown by the mother in **Part II,** to push the girl towards her *destiny* that would convince us of the mother's stated wish in **Part I** of the novel for Joanne's *destiny*; other than the fact it may have been lip-service at that time. However, throughout the novel, we see Joanne's developing characteristics as described by Gran-gran of what being *"A Woman of Destiny"* means to her in the girl's farewell. Throughout the novel, Joanne therefore achieves her ambition as Gran-gran directs: being ***tenacious, strong, use of her memory, (*****Part II*****), being steadfast, refusing to be suppressed, living pragmatically (strongly demonstrated in* Part II*) and remembering their ancestral point of contact (returning to the Grenadian landscape).***

Joanne is very much a child at the beginning of the novel, this is because she is only 10 years old and is not allowed to think for herself, but is dictated to, especially by Aunt Meena. Evidently, Joanne tells us; ***"My orders for the day were given in quick successive commands. My tasks were set and there was no arguing with that - always accepted in quiet submission, total obedience and life rolled along,"* (p.19). *"You did not cross her path, no, not at all!"* (p.19).** We are also told in ***A Woman of Destiny*** that the prevailing view of children was that ***"they should be seen and not heard,"* (p.16).** This shows the reader an extraordinary way of bringing up children.

Despite this, Joanne has developed a passion for learning, and does appear to learn from different sources: her village friends, overhearing adults in the market or at home, her best friend, Justin, her environment in England, as both an observer and a '*listener*' and she shares this through her inner thoughts with the reader.

Joanne changes and develops during the novel to become an independent thinker, to take charge of her own life. Thus she makes the decision not to pursue the quest to seek her father; having become clearer, at the end of the novel, about the reasons for his absence. In a sense, Joanne shows us that she has embraced all the characteristics of being a ***Woman of Destiny***, which Gran-gran elucidated to her at their parting. She has become someone who is self-directed, independent in her thinking, and who would select aspects of her tradition and culture that she feels are relevant to her present existence and also for her future development. Therefore, this Calypso novel, concerned with the education, development and maturing of this young protagonist, is also a *bildungsroman.*

Ann, Monica, Yvonne and Lydia

Ann, Monica, Yvonne and Lydia are Aunt Meena's children. They are presented as very subservient to Aunt Meena and as ***"children should be seen and not heard,"* (p.16)** we do not really see or hear much from them. There is a sense that Aunt Meena's children would rebel against the strict disciplinarian, who is their mother; as is evident when the girls and the narrator are caught breaking Aunt Meena's rules in the Junction late one evening. The consequence is that they are physically punished, publicly, because it's Aunt Meena's policy that those, ***"who can't hear must feel!"* (p.19)** However, they are made to speak out; with the fear from the threat of punishment, in a military style inquisition, after the "African priest" molested the girls and left the village. There is a sense that they are dutiful, as they help cook and prepare meals, without conversation; with one exception, when they were bantering the day Joanne saw her periods.

Reverend Blackman

Reverend Blackman is a Baptist Priest, who gained his qualification in Trinidad. He presides over the St. John Spiritual Baptist Church; a little concrete construction, dwarfed by the nearby, huge, imposing Catholic church in Tivoli. He is a, ***"small, dark, and bony figure was dressed in the customary long, black gown. Purple sashes, decorated with embroidered crosses at each end, hung over the gown and completed the matching mitre; which bore a similar design,"* (p.1).** He is obviously influential with an image of steadfastness, complete, ***"with his worn Bible in hand and he spoke with a seasoned voice of courage; the message from the "Good Book,"* (p.1).**

He takes a warm interest in Joanne and also endorses her as someone who will be ***"A Woman of Destiny".*** He is instrumental in her deep religious conditioning, added to by Gran-gran's insistence on her daily readings of Biblical passages from her ***"Words of Comfort."*** Rev. Blackman appears to be silent throughout the novel other than when he is performing his duty; presiding over the burial of Irene in the cemetery or conducting his Sunday morning service in church. His character represents the theme of religion in the novel, being the villager's religious leader, and who ensures that their style of worship is quite inclusive – praying aloud for everyone and everything. ***"The lame, the blind, the deaf, those in prison. Not forgetting our Sisters and Brothers by the way, those who're backsliding. Those in institutions, leaders of countries and leaders of the Gospel,"* (p.85).** We are told that, ***"The list was always long and impressive. Everyone and everything was included,"* (p.85).**

The Reverend not only prays impressively, we are also told that his, ***"prayers were always filled with spiritual fervour and with the ability to uplift the supplicants,"* (p.86).** However, as with the villagers as a whole, he was not as vigilant as he should be with the "African priest". We see him just as placatory, despite the exposure of the 'African priest,' because in his general prayers, he just asks God to, ***"walk with him, [the 'African priest'] guide his footsteps and teach him to walk in the right way,"* (p.107).** By contrast, it is the women who are rebellious in their reaction to what the 'African priest' had done.

Reverend Blackman also represents a member of the village who has achieved his *destiny,* since he was able to go out of the island and qualify as a priest in Trinidad, and then return to Grenada, as a symbol of achievement.

The Family in England

The family in England on the other hand, appears to be disconnected; seen as a whole unit, yet fragmented within. The disconnection also has something to do with distance away from the Grenadian landscape. Irene's relationship with her daughter Joanne is most clinical, and there are no tête-à-têtes between them that show the kind of bonding we are used to between Joanne and Gran-gran. Apart from the lack of warmth in their family circles, Joanne's mother and Aunty Mary's language, we are told, is not authentic, but ***"ornamental Standard English,"* (p.247)** and it's only when the women revert to a more traditional from of expression - the Grenadian Creole, ***"their emotional responses seem more natural,"* (p.247).** Joanne, it seems has moved from Grenada into a contrasting environment, where she exists as a dutiful child, doing chores and yearning for her past life in Grenada.

Calvin

Calvin, like Justin's father and the men in the Grenada rum shop, appear to be sterile, with failed ambitions. His ambitions are at odds with his responsibility as a father in

England's racist environment. Therefore, his vision for his ***destiny*** is met with rebuff and barriers at both the home and employment levels. In his frustration, he resorts to violence and is known to hit Irene when they argue. As the man in their household, Calvin has no close relationship with Joanne or the twins; preferring to be playing his guitar or going to the betting shop.

Calvin wants to be a solicitor, refuses to do menial tasks and is outspoken because, ***"he says he don't want no menial work and nobody telling him to sweep no factory floor for the hell of it," (p.247).*** However, despite having ideas about a laudable achievement for himself, (to become a solicitor), he disapproves of any plans to buy a house in England; a suggestion he views as a ***"foolish ambition, impossible by coloured standards" (p.249)*** or a ***"crazy idea" (p.250)*** which he ***"could not see happening to them in England," (p.249).***

Calvin's frustrations stems from being the man in the family, and ***"a Black man in this hell of a place" (p.250);*** who feels he has climbed down the social ladder. He was an Overseer in Grenada, who now has to resort to doing factory work in England and this presents a complicated psychology for the family in England. Therefore, when his wife tells him to ***"go to hell with his pride,"*** he lashes out and ***"slaps"*** her, ***"followed by scuffling between them," (p.250).***

They, like other migrant families in Britain, were faced with insecurities, unplanned pregnancies, faced joblessness, plagued by uprootedness; and having to deal with merciless Landlords and the pressure of supporting families left behind in Grenada, were strenuous challenges for migrant Caribbean families in Britain. Clearly, Irene and Calvin have different attitudes as to how they should progress and succeed as a family unit in England. Calvin is intolerant of situations he finds himself in and openly challenges them. Similar to Justin's dad in Grenada, Calvin is a tragic figure whose present lifestyle is at odds with his ambitions and neutered ***destiny.***

Aunty Mary

Unlike Calvin and Irene, her sister Aunty Mary, has been living in England for a much longer time. We are told that she was ***"placatory,"*** who ***"saw her role as constantly reasoning with her anxious sister over her niece's chosen path for the future," (p.291).*** Aunty Mary helped Irene to remain steadfast by suggesting she joined a *Susu* for economic survival. She is the one Joanne went to regarding her confusion about making a **"High Tea"** menu for her school homework.

Aunty Mary empowers Irene to think about progressing by buying a house in England and helps to maintain a sense of togetherness, as they share a kind of folk wisdom. The opposite would be ***"dog eating [Irene's] share" (p.248)*** said in the proverbial wisdom of the folks, as they knit and talk. Her reasoning is logical as she too, has had to learn from mistakes, like Irene. ***"We used to t'ink England life easy. Yes, we all want to be something great but we have to live, eat, and survive firs', " (p.248).***

She assists her sister in finding links to employment for Calvin, in order to avert a domestic disaster, with her ***"do it now"*** attitude. ***"The women had begun to find answers to their problems, and intent on working immediately on their expressed resolutions, Aunty Mary took the lead," (p.249).*** She is a bridge-builder who represents stability. Her image is similar to Gran-gran; quietly advising, suggesting, guiding, and she is proactive. After Irene's death, she is the one who finally helps Joanne fit the pieces to her life's puzzles together, with her explanations at the end of the novel; about what took place between Randolph and Irene in their youth.

The Twins

Darris and Dareen are first generation British-Caribbean children who were born in England. They do not seem to have any other connection with the Caribbean landscape, and seem disconnected even within their own immediate family circle. Their behaviour confirms their lack of emotional support for their mother, even when she was gravely ill in hospital. We do not see them at the burial in Grenada, so it's ironic that Dareen has gone off to be a missionary to help others abroad, when she does not appear to practice charity at home. Notwithstanding this, at the end of the novel, Irene leaves everything she owns to them in a Will and deliberately leaves Joanne out of it.

Irene

Irene appears to have a closer bond with the twins, as it is the last names uttered on her lips, when she ignored Joanne, at her bedside. ***"She stirred first then opened her eyes. She looked at me, asked for Darrin and Darris, then went back to sleep," (p.299).*** This left the narrator to conclude that her inclusion in the family was as incidental as her life had been - an ***"existence of convenience" (p. 299).*** This makes Irene a tragic figure, who was not able to reconcile the mistakes of her past, lacks forgiveness and who appears to project those feelings of hatred for her aborted ***destiny,*** unto Joanne.

The narrator, it seems, wanted to believe otherwise but when faced with the reality of rejection, it had a devastating effect on Joanne, she was able to finally let go: ***"…something in mum's eyes caused that firmly rooted feeling to shake. That had gone beyond me, into a deep unknown. It had caused a feeling of abandonment, a sense of déjà-vu; an uncanny sense of unease that I had felt and experienced before. I felt cold, not unusual for a March evening, but it caused a tugging at my heart, like a snap of a long, taut piece of string, which had been straining, stretching to breaking point, but had now snapped," (299).***

Irene resented Randolph and his family's new-found interest in Joanne at the age of 12 and feels it is somehow too late for them to strike up a relationship, underpinned by her reasoning that Joanne is ***"now she's big enough to give me a cup of water," (p.169)*** it's not necessary for their involvement. She refers to Randolph and his family as ***"good-for-nothings" (p.209)*** and her proverbial expression relates the depths of her feelings, ***"What's not good in the morning cant' be good in the night;" (p.169)*** meaning they were not good enough for her at the beginning, so they may as well stay out of her live!. She expresses her reasons for this with the fact that ***"leopards cannot change their***

***spots,"* (p.169)** they must remain as they are – disconnected. There is therefore a no-turning-back rule, where Irene and Randolph are concerned and ultimately, this includes Joanne.

However, unlike her husband Calvin, she is more tolerant of the difficulties they experience in their marriage, and is willing to push boundaries to deal with their situations with a "can do" and "do it now" attitude. This threatens Calvin's masculinity to the point where he feels compelled to remind Irene that he is ***"the man in the house,"* (p251).** Irene takes the 'lead' by joining a ***Susu,*** (a cultural form of banking), and daring to talk about plans for buying a house in England without referring to him, usurps his Authority and undermines his masculinity.

Irene had learnt to take on a leadership role in her job; a situation which caused problems for her at work, between Rose and the other General Assistants. Her capability is therefore seen as a threat, as she does not appear to baulk at any situation she finds herself in; for example, bringing up her 3 daughters on her own.

We learn a good deal about Irene from her letters to her sister, Aunt Meena, in Grenada and can conclude that as a complex figure, she has had to endure a great deal of suffering from an early age. Irene had envisioned a planned marriage as part of her '***destiny***;' ***"to make things look respectable,"* (p.169)** which would have ***"made up for the shame"* (p.208)** she had brought on her family; especially the fact that, ***"Even before she [Joanne] was well formed in my belly, those nastiness did reject her,"* (p.169).** Additionally, in England she had a miscarriage, despite having birth control in place and continues to live fearfully of Landlords. She has a husband who has ambitions which do not match the reality of their situation at home, and as the sole breadwinner, takes courses of actions which appear to offend him.

Ultimately, it's what Irene says that shows us her complex make-up. This tragic figure displays impulses that show a level of repression; which gives rise to her abnormal or pathological behavior. The narrator tells us that Irene's death, ***"revealed a web of deception, mixed with anger, and the need to wreak pain and havoc on those she considered responsible for her life's dilemmas. Bundles of letters, many unopened but carefully preserved, were discovered in her original suitcase,"* (p.305).**

We are told that the original suitcase from 1960 contained, ***"many items in the box inside that grip had the answers to many of my questions,"* (p.305)** which included ***"scores of letters, addressed to me from Emma. There were also letters to me from past boyfriends and most importantly to mum from Randolph addressed from America,"* (p.305).** Thus, the quest would probably not have been necessary, and this tends to support Joanne's ultimate decision to abort her search for Randolph and instead continue to create her own *destiny*.

However, whatever view we take of Irene, it is what she says to explain her actions that express the strength of her feelings, the depths of her burdens and her complex psychology; ***"I always have the feelings that maybe that's what killed Papa, who***

knows? All the same, it's a heavy cross to bear," (p.169). It's the first time there is reference to a father-figure in the girls' lives and her suppressed feelings of loss is quite poignant.

Education

The theme of education presented in the novel is tied up with harshness, violence, domination, passivity, and information that seem unclear in its colonial style of teaching. There is no doubt that children and their parents are recipients of a colonial education. Justin's dad confirms his love of literature, being able to recite **Wordsworth, Shakespeare** and **Blake**'s poetry, and intimates that he understands etymology, phonology, syntax, prosody; though they cause ***"confusion in his head," (p.49).*** As a child, Joanne is unable to make sense of her **"*rousing war-time songs*" (p.)** especially "**Men of Harlech**", the content of which was anachronistic to her in the island. Joanne remembers certain lines from the lyrics of this song, which is in fact, Nineteenth Century lyrics from Joseph Barnby, commonly sung in America from 1784:

Men of Harlech! In the Hollow,
Do ye hear like rushing billow
Wave on wave that surging follow
Battle's distant sound?
Tis the tramp of Saxon foemen,
Saxon spearmen, Saxon bowmen,
Be they knights or hinds or yeomen,
They shall bite the ground!
Loose the folds asunder,
Flag we conquer under!
The placid sky now bright on high,
Shall launch its bolts in thunder!
Onward! 'tis the country needs us,
He is bravest, he who leads us
Honor's self now proudly heads us,
Freedom, God and Right!

Rocky Steeps and passes narrow,
Flash with spear and flight of arrow
Who would think of death or sorrow?
Death is glory now!
Hurl the reeling horsemen over,
Let the earth dead foemen cover
Fate of friend, of wife, of lover,
Trembles on a blow!
Strands of life are riven!
Blow for blow is given
In deadly lock, or battle shock,
And mercy shrieks to heaven!
Men of Harlech! Young or hoary,
Would you win a name in story?
Stike for home, for life, for glory!
Freedom, God and Right!

According to Data Wales, "*The song Men of Harlech is something of an unofficial anthem in Wales. Every Welsh person knows the tune and despite the variety of lyrics over the years, the martial air has become identified with the country's determination to retain its identity. Harlech Castle in north Wales, one of the "iron ring" of castles intended to subdue Wales in medieval times, remains as a picturesque reminder of the ultimate futility of the invader's ambition."* [2]

Therefore, based on the sentiments of the song being sung in the Caribbean environment, it is no wonder that no one, including Aunt Meena and Gran-gran, could offer any information beyond the fact that men from all over the island answered the call to fight with British soldiers on behalf of their ***"King and Country."*** This reference is made to

World War II, during the reign of King George. It is obvious that these lyrics were used to conjure the spirit of the defending the British realm, as it did for the Men of Harlech in defending Harlech Castle in the fifteenth century; a reality that was very far removed from the Caribbean environment.

Later, we hear about the preparations being made for a visit from the Queen and the Duke, from a Calypso, which roused and excited the population in the ***"dress rehearsals."*** The role of the Calypsonian here is to function as the ***"peoples' newspaper,"*** influencing thought and behaviour, so it is not surprising that, ***"The island was in an upheaval and Calypsonians sang, spurring the people on, increasing the tempo, giving the low-down and spreading the gospel,"* (p.71).**

This provides confirmation that the political masters in charge of the island are indeed British. In this scenario, a portrait of the Queen and the Union Jack being prominent in school, confirmed their position. Additionally, Mr. Jessup, the ex-army General Headmaster of the local school, perpetuates colonialism on a day-to-day basis, as he relishes his ***"delicious"*** role, drilling the ***"children-soldiers, taking the Left right! Left right beat and command, before the resounding "TENTION!"* (p.70).** Ultimately, there is a question of "relevance" of the education being provided to the island's population. However, this question has perhaps already been answered due to pre-independence preparations taking place in Grenada. Interestingly, in this approaching dispensation, people are given a ***choice*** for the first time, to write the island's national anthem. The word ***"choice"*** is significant, since the population has, for a considerable length of time, been forced to accept imposition and domination from outsiders to date.

Migration

Perhaps the person most critical of the effect of colonial education, though he did not openly intend to do so, is Justin's dad. There is a sense that most of the villagers end up working on the land, what he calls ***"below the cocoa"* (p.38).** He advises his son to avoid this and advocates a constant engagement with his ***"books."*** It means that to date, some villagers feel they have had little success in education per se, and we know that many left the island to seek betterment abroad. Therefore, success and advancement is not associated with lifestyles ***within*** but ***outside*** the island. The image is also that advancement and success equate with 'escape' and migration.

Like other Caribbean islanders, many Grenadians left the island to seek a better life elsewhere. It is estimated, from census data, that the number of Grenadian-born migrants in other parts of the Caribbean and in First World countries, equal that of the number of people (110,000), living in the island. Popular destinations include New York, Toronto, Montreal, Britain and Australia.

This is why Emma, Joanne, Emery and others are '*children in waiting;*' preparing to escape the harsh realities of working life in the Grenadian landscape. Additionally, judging from each parent's plan and expectation for their children's success or ***"destiny,"*** their view of success is tied up with having a good education – Joanne's mother told her at the age of 6 to ***"learn good in school,"* (p.28);** Gran-gran on the other hand, makes her do so actively, as Joanne reads daily to her from her ***'Words of Comfort'*** book. Justin's dad publicly derides those who work on the land and expects Justin to excel with a laudable sense of ***destiny***; by becoming a lawyer. Both Justin's dad and Irene have failed at their attempts to excel in their projected education, so we could say that their sense of ***"destiny"*** was curtailed. Their extenuating circumstances made their concerns for their children more acute than concerns for themselves.

However, as we learn with Calvin and Irene, as well as Aunty Mary's experiences in England, the ***"El dorado"*** they sought, turned out to be a myth. The streets are not paved with gold. Instead, Aunty Mary sums up migrants' predicament thus; ***"We used to t'ink England life easy. Yes, we all want to be something great but we have to live, eat, and survive firs',"* (p.248).** Their situation is precarious so they have to consider themselves lucky, if they find a job. Aunt Irene's letters to her sister Meena in Grenada, outline their individual predicament also; ***"The truth is, I really didn't plan to settle long here,"* (p.167).** Irene's purpose of migration was to achieve something abroad and then return to Grenada; just as other villagers, the Reverend Blackman and Mr. Mitchell had done in Trinidad and England respectively.

Irene also describes the harshness of working-life in England; ***"eating late at night after work and going straight to sleep, too tired to let the food settle before sleeping,"* (p.167).** In a discussion between Aunty Mary and Irene we are told; ***"Landlords, it was commonly known, ..., or were nervous of aspiring coloured people; ....those who didn't want to settle down to just any job but want to climb the ladder of success,"* (p.246).** As a result, the migrants express a sense of regret; ***"Some of us used to think England had a money-tree, but now reality hit home, you work or starve,"* (p.246).**

Calvin is not working, and the conflict created is when Irene takes matters in her own hands, to avoid 'starving,' he walks out on his family. Faced with the above dilemmas, he is unable to maintain his family unit without feeling that his ***destiny*** is stillborn. Additionally, based on the above sentiments, his outburst against English Landlords' perspectives of what he should accept is therefore not unfounded.

Violence

It is perhaps the imagery of the macabre, when Itran's severed head is paraded through the streets, as well as the Headmaster's level of violence, when he meted out corporal punishment to the Joanne and Emma, which really highlight the theme of violence in the novel. Joanne and Emma's way of coping with the impact that the severe public punishment had on them, was to adopt the ***"grinning mask,"* p.58).** There is a sense that the use of the word ***"mask"*** is used as a concealer, or as a guard that blocks out the girls' repressed psychological pain.

In ***A Woman of Destiny,*** physical punishment is endorsed by the State, and as a result, it is perpetuated in the village in different ways. The school Headmaster administers ***corporal punishment*** with a ***leather belt*** in front of his 500 student population. Aunt Meena metes out punishment with a ***big stick*** to her girls in public on the street at the Junction, in the village. Calvin ***slaps*** Irene at home (in England), when he is frustrated, and Dessima and Jean ***slap, bite and attack*** each other in a public brawl on the streets in the village. Violence of the most macabre kind is seen when Sukram ***chops off Itran's head*** and parades it in the village streets.

There is a sense here that violence is seen a way of dealing with extreme grief, and emotional and psychological difficulties. Evidently, Sukram seems to trivialise the enormity of the incident with Itran when he says, ***"I catch a big fish today,"*** **(p.36).** Calvin on the other hand, ***slaps*** Irene, which escalates into a ***scuffle*** at home, when he is frustrated with their domestic situation in England. Additionally, the women would have ***killed*** the "African priest" with their cutlasses and failing this, an extreme level of verbal ***violence was manifested in their language*** when they cursed the 'priest' in his absence.

Therefore, several levels of violence are perpetuated in society and can be defined as follows:

1. **Physical force**: effecting and intended to effect pain or injuries: the Headmaster
2. **Powerful, untamed, or devastating force**: Sukram's murder
3. **Great strength of feeling, as in language**: the fervour of the women's curses on the 'African priest'
4. **An unjust, unwarranted, or unlawful display of force**: the women's public brawl intending to intimidate, quite unknown to the person they were supposed to be fighting over!
5. **Intention to violate**: the African priest and the girls
6. **Physical force used to inflict injury**: Calvin as well as Aunt Meena

The imagery of violence perpetuating violence is presented in a subtle way that the Author may be suggesting that the violence in the novel carries over from the physical and psychic violence committed against the race as a whole, beginning with the slave trade; that are still perpetuated on a number of levels in society. By interweaving allusions to the Colonial Headmaster into her story with a neutral tone, this just lets the information speak for itself.

Storytelling

An important aspect of the Grenadian culture is the tradition of story-telling, with folk tales bearing both African and French influences. The character Anancy is a spider that is a trickster, originated from West Africa, and is prevalent on other islands as well. French influence can be seen in ***La Diablesse***, a well-dressed she-devil, and ***Ligaroo*** (from ***Loup Garoux***), a werewolf.

The storytelling tradition is a major focus, in *A Woman of Destiny*, as it emulates the oral form, in presenting the story which Joanne is telling the reader, though in a written format. Also subsumed within the novel's framework are the myriad other stories about the lives of the other characters, (presented as narrated songs e.g. ***solos, duos, trios*** or ***group percussionists***), as they too ***tell it like it is.***

In *A Woman of Destiny,* there is a suggestion that not only Anancy stories are folk stories. There is a sense that anything which takes place in the island and is passed on by oral transmission, could be inscribed in the storytelling culture as folk wisdom. For example, both the *Hurricane Janet* and *Cosmos and his father* stories can be seen as '*Authorized*' folk tales, given a *rite de passage* in the novel by Gran-gran and Aunt Meena. This is because the stories are told to the children in the storytelling manner of folktales being passed on. Therefore, whether fact or fiction, they become the stories of the folks that are transmitted from generation to generation. That being the case, Joanne's story, *"A Woman of Destiny,"* is inscribed as her story but also that of the folks and is also embodied in the story-telling tradition.

Characters

Gran-gran – She is instrumental in helping to create Joanne's cultural memory via both group and individual routes. Individually, **she represents ancestral wisdom and carries within her a family lineage of memory,** which she acknowledges is important and necessary in cultivating success. She teaches Joanne about the efficacy of the herbs and medicinal benefits of the bush and spices from the landscape. She imparts knowledge about various icons around the home (the mortar, pestle, grinding stone and mule's saddle, stories of the family descendants – her Ashanti warrior mother, **Hurricane Janet,** Brer Anancy and Cosmos Stories). She gives Joanne beads from her great grand-mother to be used as a point of contact; in order to recall and remember their benefits to her. In other words, Gran-gran advocates that Joanne should use her memory as an ancestral bridge-builder, in order to maintain a strong sense of self; to inspire diligence and steadfastness in achieving her ***destiny.***

As the elder and matriarch in the family, Gran-gran carries within her the sum total of Grenadian culture, which she is expected to transmit to successive generations and we see this in the storytelling tradition that she and Aunt Meena pass on to the children. She also uses memory to instill caution and good sense, as well as to guide Joanne, when she retells her rape story. Gran-gran is instrumental in helping Joanne to develop a specific memory database from her *Words of Comfort*, which Joanne is expected to recall and activate at the appropriate time of need. This is evidence of the personal and social process of making things memorable.

On one hand, it means we have the ability to create the quality of memory we want for our future needs, and select our responses to stimuli that trigger memory recall. On the other hand, one of Gran-gran's personal memory experiences demonstrates that there is an aspect of memory which we seem to have no control over. These are memories that originate from traumatic experiences, that lay deeply buried in our mind and resurrect when certain painful stimuli trigger them; causing them to surface at will. Examples are Gran-gran's rape, Irene's rejection by Randolph and his family, her miscarriage, and Joanne's mother's rejection of her. Additionally, as Joanne undergoes training from Gran-gran, she is told that memory is essential. Joanne must remember Gran-gran's farewell guidance, in order to activate the characteristics which will enable her to achieve her ***destiny*** or failing to do so, will run the risk of failure.

Irene – Her character evidences the fact **that memory represents ongoing problems based on pain that she suffered in the past.** It therefore means that without memory there is no pain; if you cannot remember physical pain then you cannot be plagued by regret or grief. It also means that you cannot suffer pain if you cannot remember the events that hurt you.

However, Irene's memory of her past, personal shame, which according to Aunty Mary, was seen as "a disaster;" (becoming pregnant at the age of 15, Randolph's denial that he was the father and his parents rejection of their relationship, her daily 'burden' that it may all have been the result of her father's untimely death and the reality of bringing a bastard child into the world under those circumstances); were instances of personal, painful, memory that had multiple and conflicting manifestations that seem to wrestle with Irene's mind; making that psychic space a disturbed one. Added to these, are her further failed attempts at home-making with Calvin, (who walked out on her and their children) and the daily, racist rejection she suffered in the workplace, made Irene a significant sufferer.

At the end of the novel, Joanne discovers the truth about hers and Irene's past; hidden in the many unopened letters which Irene had collected and kept, as well as the complex pathology evidenced in her behaviour – overt rejection of Joanne and deliberately leaving her out of her **Will,** and instead favouring Joanne's younger siblings. Irene's coping strategy of dealing with a painful and eventful past was an attempt to bury it, or lock it out of her life. However, there is a sense that if Irene was able to articulate those mishaps or put them into a story, it is possible that in time this could have been transformed into moments of triumph, hope and guidance to her daughter; instead of the terror, regret and bitterness she displayed. For example, in contrast to Irene, Gran-gran's occasional nervous twitching shows signs of resurrected pain and hurt. However, she used her rape story as an example of caution and guidance for Joanne, triumphant with hope that a repetition is less likely.

Irene's story is one that shows us how, when we suffer loss, we also have the propensity for renewal and healing, in order to obtain coherence and meaning through what we remember and tell. We see her using this strategy when she tells Darris about her past miscarriage, in order to warn the girl of possible risks and dangers in the outside world, once Darris had made up her mind to leave home. Therefore, had Irene adopted such a strategy to deal with the "disaster" she endured with becoming pregnant, the corresponding sense of 'loss' and 'incoherence' which Joanne experienced and which dominated her early life, could have been avoided.

Joanne – Being a child at the beginning of the novel, **memory is shown to be essential for Joanne's growth** and its importance is demonstrated mainly in Gran-gran's relationship with her. Gran-gran takes a practical approach to ensuring Joanne understands the value of memory as well as remembering, and educates her culturally, traditionally, and socially on all aspects of life as lived in Grenada. Having suffered painful memories herself, she takes steps to ensure that Joanne does not fall foul to instances that could needlessly duplicate suffering.

- Therefore, in order to avoid such pitfalls, Joanne is taught the **story telling tradition** to instill caution, good sense and provide historical knowledge to hers and the village children, so that they could learn about and remember their past.

- Joanne is taught about the herbs, medicinal bush and how to apply them for healthy living. Gran-gran uses these to instill the value of memory and remembering of all that the **natural landscape** has to offer by teaching Joanne the details.

- Joanne is empowered to remember as she gets older, with an eye set firmly on a projected successful ***destiny***; examples of **role-models** that she should emulate are shown to her by Gran-gran. This is also linked to symbolic iconic relics that have meaning in both the past and present.

- Joanne is helped to understand the process of memory formation and recollection by creating **ancestral linkages** via the information about her great grandmother and the characteristics of warrior-hood, as passed on in Joanne's farewell guidance on the qualities needed for achieving ***destiny.***

These are positive memory formation and would make for happy recollection. However, Joanne has had some unpleasant personal memories that could cause interconnected problems in shaping her sense of self. Justin's dad's made a negative pronouncement on her abilities, when she attempted to take part in the national anthem competition. Experience of the 'African priest' molestation among the village girls, the subtle and overt racism experienced over the Caravan Hire fiasco, discovering she not only has an absent father but secrecy and shame connected with her entry into the world, and discovering her mother's rejection of her, makes Joanne a significant sufferer also.

Migrating to England and experiencing the differences between the two landscapes, gave Joanne a wellspring of reflection, imagination, recollection and use of her memory in ways that being in the Grenadian landscape only could not offer her. For Joanne, memory of her Grenadian landscape, whilst living in England, provided a range of emotions – at times there was tension, regret, nostalgia, attempts to recreate her cultural identity in her 'new' environment and moments of triumph, when she overcame those challenges. Joanne used her past group-memory to reshape and impose her shared sense of group identity in the English landscape when her group went on holiday in the West Country. Having learnt how memory could be utilized positively, she states in **Chapter 13; "*Gran-gran had taught me to be strong at all times and I had held on to her advice***

***and personal words of comfort, just as I had held on to the three beads she had given me,"* (p.299).**

It was therefore not surprising, that Gran-gran's farewell advice to Joanne as she prepared to leave Grenada, was mostly about remembering; and the value of memory was endorsed as essential in achieving a successful ***destiny.*** Consequently, at the end of the novel, Joanne tells us of the benefit she gained from her application of memory and the use of her three beads, in her new environment; ***"they had inspired me to accept what to others seemed unacceptable, held visions of goals and aims thought impossible to achieve by others. Above all they had bought a sense of inexplicable strength, unshakeable determination to get ahead, and an unwavering drive to accomplish Gran-gran's long term goals for my life – to get to the top, no matter what!"* (p.299)**

Aunty Mary – Although she has been in England the longest, the character who quietly holds on to **Group/collective memory** is Aunty Mary. She maintains a sense of the group by ensuring Irene joins a ***Su-su*** run by Mrs. Matthew. This is one of the oldest forms of folk banking performed by villagers which involves one person who is elected to collect a specific sum of money from a number of people who form a group and promise to submit their money, (e.g. weekly) into a pool, when the total amount is collected for that week. This total amount is given in turn to each member of the group, on a weekly basis, until everyone has had a turn to get the total sum of money. Then the whole process begins again. Aunty Mary instructs Irene to join a ***Su-su*** to ensure she and her family's economic survival during the period of her husband's (Calvin) unemployment.

Aunt Mary is similar to Gran-gran; quietly advising, suggesting, guiding, and she is proactive and she uses her memory of the details to finally help Joanne to fit the pieces to her life's jig-saw puzzle together; when she explained what took place between Randolph and Irene. Aunty Mary also empowers Irene to think about economic advancement by buying a house in England. Her character helps to maintain a sense of togetherness or collective experience, as she instigates the sharing of folk wisdom. Notice her language; **"*dog eating dog or Irene's share*" (p248),** said in the proverbial wisdom of the folks, as both she and Irene knit and discuss. Proverbs and parables are typically used by the older folks to instill folk wisdom, caution and good sense.

The Importance of "Memory" in *Woman of Destiny*

As humans, we have the capacity to remember things: information, actions, and then to recall these when we want to think on them or adjust and re-adjust them accordingly. Universally, this is understood as our memory.

However, parts of our memory may be hidden from us in our subconscious; and can be recalled unconsciously without our wanting them to, or we recall them consciously when we want to remember something specifically. Generally, it would be fair to say that we share a common understanding of what memory is, whether it's private or public; and this may be defined as follows:

- **Memory is the act of remembering or recollecting** events from the past.
- In some cases, past events come back to haunt us, or happy memories help to **brighten our days or lift up our spirits from sadness or moments of despair**. (*Personal and group*).
- **Memory defines our sense of self and distinguishes who we are**; especially our sense of being a separate and distinct person. (*Personal memory*).
- **Memory is remembrance of collective activities and gatherings of peoples** and **ideas**; (G*roup memory*). In other words, memory has a social role as it helps to shape our sense of the group, through our shared experiences.
- **Memory plays an important role in character development** and in ***A Woman of Destiny****;* it is instrumental in the progression of the plot.

In *A Woman of Destiny*, Cultural memory plays a specific role in reflecting our cultural make-up and becomes the template through which we can define our cultural identity; wherever we are located around the globe. Also culturally in the novel, memories are formed by social, political, and religious events in the lives of characters and have a bearing on their past. These therefore highlight the complexity of memory; as it can inspire a range of emotions so clearly that it cannot be one single thing.

In *A Woman of Destiny,* it is possible to see memory from three distinct viewpoints; often these exist separately and concurrently in the text.

Firstly, memory establishes a feeling of nostalgia in a text. **Secondly**, and most universally, it is used as a method of constructing both individual and cultural identity. T**hirdly,** in inviting us to remember, memory embodies both sorrow and triumph. This means that when we remember sad events, it acts as a reminder of how we suffered loss. For some, that loss can be softened over time and for those who are unable to cope with its complexity, it causes pathological behaviour (Irene) that can be equally baffling. But the act of remembering can also create a story which relieves sadness and enables us to be triumphant. (*Gran-gran's telling of her rape episode to Joanne and Mr. McDonald's demise as well as Joanne's own story throughout the text).* All three perspectives above demonstrate that we have the capacity to carry the past within us, wherever we go. Therefore, it can be resurrected at intervals, based on particular circumstances that trigger remembrance.

Our faculty of remembrance and speech enables us to tell stories. We construct and maintain our individual, as well as collective lives through remembering. Consequently, memory in *A Woman of Destiny* raises important issues about the relationship between personal experience and its retelling via the narrator. Joanne is presented as a credible witness of events, through which her memory is presented as a documentary of evidence in this novel. However, within the text we are able to see the different levels of remembering and the impact this has on each character's decision and subsequent action in the text. For different characters, memory can be seen to have a number of conflicting characteristics that compete for recognition; ultimately proving that memory is a complex thing.

Grenadian Migrant Children: The position of the migrant children in England is an interesting one. Similar to Joanne, we see the group of friends who came from the tropical landscape, attempting to **remember by relocating their cultural identity** in England's landscape as they remember it to be. They choose a place that resembles Grenada's natural landscape by remembering because; ***"Dave said that it reminded him of life in Grenada."*** Notice that memory is the key to choice, ***"something to do with the green landscape, driving up and down the Cornish hills and the thick darkness at nights, not to mention the narrow country lanes with matted, stubbly bush on either side,"* (p.286).**

Here was the group's attempt to project cultural identity in England, by laying claim to the territory or space. It helped them to ***"relish the idea of using torches and seeing the real sky with stars at night,"* (p.286). We are also told that they *"attempted to have mock storytelling but nothing came as close to the real thing in Grenada,"* (p.346).** It is also the act of remembering their past cultural landscape they are able to conclude that the West Country's ***"darkness was menacing and was not conducive to sustaining the "crick-crack" storytelling framework,"* (p.286).**

- Memory here is defining who those children are, because it helps to **define their sense of self and distinguishes who they are i.e.,** Grenadian migrant children.
- Memory is also operating here **as remembrance of collective activities** and gatherings of peoples and ideas in their past; (***Group memory***). In other words, **memory in its social role** is helping to shape their sense of the group, through their shared experiences.

However, the migrant Grenadian children had come to realize that adaptation and memory has to work hand-in-hand, if it is to define their cultural identity in the new environment. They were aware that, ***"we had all been deluded into the belief that everything in the "garden" called England was rosy,"* (p269)** especially their childish role-playing and high expectations of life in England. Joan states, such high expectations of England were ***"farcical, but we could not have known it – no one could, children or adults,"* (p.269).** Therefore, coming to terms with their new "***home***" or landscape necessitated creating an expansion of their group experience. This involves utilizing knowledge of their past memory and using strategies that help them to create new memories. They do so by ***"venturing into other parts of England,"* (p.269)** they knew little of.

Children of migrant parents born in England: Additionally, for some within the group, we are told had ***"lived all of their lives"* (p.269)** in England; meaning that some of them were born in England and their intention is therefore to ***"enjoy our home,"***

(p.269). It is noteworthy that those who were born in England would **create memory of a first generation migrant group.** Their process of creating memory would be firstly the recreated cultural identity they share with the Grenadian migrant children, as they focus on the memories they create themselves by social, political, and religious events in their lives. This does begin to show the impact of different kinds of memory and its implication for those in the Diaspora; the result is a complexity of the notion of memory, since it cannot be one single thing. This would have a wider frame of reference for memory, if these children, like Christopher, find themselves back in the Grenadian landscape.

Diaspora

The word **diaspora** (from ***Greek diaspeirō***), means **"*I scatter*"** or **"*I spread about;*"** is defined as the scattering of a population with a common background, from a smaller geographical region, which moves from its original homeland to dispersions in other geographical areas. The dispersion can be due to mass movement of an **involuntary** nature, as in the case of the African Trans-Atlantic slave trade, Indentured Indians from South Asia, imperialist expansion; expulsion (Jews from Judea), or **voluntary human migration** of people from one place to another, with the intention of settling temporarily or permanently in the new location.

But nowadays, the word ***diaspora*** can be applied to almost any population on the move referring to the specific context of their existence. For example, ***corporate diaspora*** has been used for professional communities of individuals who are working away from their homeland; ***science diaspora***, for communities of scientists who conduct their research away from their homeland, and so the descriptive conception has become an expanding term. Scholars have come to identify different groups living away from their homeland, based on their nationality e.g. ***African* diaspora**, ***Caribbean* diaspora**, ***European* diaspora** and so on. The word ***diaspora*** is also a subject of study which is now an academic field that was established in the late 20th century. Its main aim is to study ethnic populations, called **"*Diaspora peoples,*"** who are dispersed due to slavery, racism, war, or national conflict.

Generally, the movement is over very long distances and may involve individuals (e.g. Grenadian migrants in ***A Woman of Destiny***), whole family units (indentured South Indian workers to the Caribbean) or in large groups e.g. trafficking in human beings and ethnic cleansing. Most diaspora communities maintain strong ties with their homeland, often referred to as **"*back home;*"** have thoughts of returning one day (Irene), have relationships with other communities also in their diaspora; may not integrate into the host-country; or on the other hand, may attempt to do so with varying consequences.

In fact, some individuals may have multiple homes – both in the diaspora and their **"*back home,*"** with different reasons for maintaining both. As is noted in ***A Woman of Destiny***, diasporic cultural development often follow a different course from the original population and over time (e.g. Peter, Darris, Darrin); this tends to vary the original cultural practices, traditions, language and other factors, including religion. In ***A Woman*** *of Destiny,* Peter shows no allegiance to Caribbean culture or traditions and makes it quite clear why he wants to marry outside of the black race.

This section of the **Study Guide** is entitled **Diaspora** because it documents several issues in ***A Woman of Destiny,*** to do with the movement of peoples from one country (Grenada) to settle in the other (England) for economic and other reasons. There are also references to Grenadians migrating to America e.g. Emery who was waiting to join his parents there and Justin's dad's childhood friend, who immigrated to the USA and is now a lawyer. We also learn that Manny, Christopher's dad and Velma's partner; had emigrated from Jamaica and also that migrants from other Caribbean islands lived or congregated together at weekends. Gran-Gran's mother, we are told, was an Ashanti warrior from Africa, and her son had migrated to England where he later died under questionable circumstances.

The **Grenadian diaspora** is significant in the novel, as it documents geographical, economic, and political history of both Grenada and England, in ways that relate directly to their social and cultural history; based on their personal experiences. Looking at the history of the movement of peoples from Grenada has a direct bearing on the island's history of human migration, as it affected the lives of the characters.

Consequently, there is correlation between the characters' personal movement to the diaspora and to world history. This makes the subject of diaspora in ***A Woman of Destiny*** important to study. Therefore, based on world historic events, we see waves of different diasporic movements taking place within the novel with push and pull factors as follows:

AFRICAN DIASPORA - FROM AFRICA TO THE CARIBBEAN:

Ashanti warrior – slave, (Gran-gran's mother). One of the largest diaspora in history is the African Diaspora. This dates back to several centuries, with its **Trans-Atlantic Slave Trade of transporting 9 to 12 million people from North, West, West-Central and South-east Africa across the globe in the Western Hemisphere as slaves.** This population and their descendants, dispersed into what was referred to as the New World, were very influential in their colonies, dominated mainly by their English, French, Italian, Portuguese and Spanish colonial masters. What is relevant in ***A Woman of Destiny*** is the confirmation of this historic input from Gran-gran, the narrator's grandmother, who has lived through two eras of colonial rule in Grenada (French and English). As a result she is able to speak **French Creole** and **English Creole**, as are those of her age group, e.g. Miss Cleothilda.

BORN IN GRENADA/THE CARIBBEAN:

- Gran-gran – Caribbean - slave parents – ***1st generation***
- Irene, Aunty Mary, Aunt Meena, villagers – ***2nd generation***
- Joanne, Emma, Justin, Claudette, Dessima, Jean and village children – ***3rd generation***

CARIBBEAN DIASPORA – THE MOVE TO ENGLAND

(i). ***VOLUNTARY MIGRATION*** **AS ECONOMIC MIGRANTS.**
Irene, Aunty Mary, Aunt Meena, Mr. Mitchell, Joanne, Emma, Jessica.

(ii). ***VOLUNTARY MIGRATION*** **– TO SUPPORT WARFARE & CONFLICT** – The West India Regiment

Within the Caribbean as a whole, the 20th century saw huge segments of the population moving to Britain, seen as the ***"Motherland."*** This was at the behest of the English government that British subjects in the colonies should respond to **the call support the war effort; on the condition that they would retain the status of British Subjects, to live in freedom under the protection of the British Crown.** The response was the formation of the **West India Regiment** – with volunteer soldiers from around the entire Caribbean region was involved.

In ***A Woman of Destiny***, we see the young Joanne trying to grapple with the meaning of the British war time song, ***Men of Harlech***, and questioning its relevance to them. Aunt Meena and Gran-gran were vague about where the song had come from and what it means but remembered the fact that West Indian soldiers throughout the Caribbean region going off to fight in the war against Germany in order to defend Britain, the ***"Motherland."***

The West India Regiment - World War I

The West India Regiment was an infantry unit of the British Army, made up of recruited Caribbean volunteers and stationed in the British colonies of the Caribbean between 1795 and 1927. This regiment was different from similar forces created in other parts of the British Empire because it formed an integral part of the regular British Army. In 1958, when the islands of the Caribbean (West Indies) formed a **Federation of the West Indies**, the West India regiment was revived with three established battalions.

This was short-lived, as it was disbanded four years later in 1962. However, throughout its existence, the West India regiment was involved in many campaigns in the West Indies and Africa, and took part in the First World War, when it served in the Middle East and East Africa. At the same time, there was also a continuous presence of small groups of students from Africa and the Caribbean slowly migrating into London.

African-Caribbean volunteer soldiers of the West India Regiment on the Somme, September 1916.

The West India Regiment - World War II

Another period of Caribbean migration to Britain was during World War II. West Indians settled in communities in London, Liverpool and around Britain; having arrived as wartime workers, merchant seaman, and servicemen from the army, navy, and air forces. For example, in February 1941, it is known that at least 345 West Indians came to work in munitions factories in and around Liverpool. After World War II, the largest influx of Black people arrived in Britain were mostly from the British West Indies; (***colonies owned by Britain***). **Over a quarter of a million West Indians came as British Subjects**; the overwhelming majority of them from Jamaica.

In the mid-1960s, the relevant period in ***A Woman of Destiny***, Britain had one of the largest overseas populations of West Indians. However, just over a decade before this date, one of the first major groups of Caribbean migrants to the UK in 1948, arrived on a ship known as **HMT *Empire Windrush***.

HMT *Empire Windrush* was a passenger liner and cruise ship launched in Germany in 1930. The United Kingdom acquired this cruise ship as a prize of war at the end of World War II and it served mainly as a British troop ship until March 1954. The ship sank in the Mediterranean Sea after it caught fire, losing four of its crew.

HMT Empire Windrush

The ***Empire Windrush***, as it's popularly called, is remembered today for bringing one of the first large groups of post-war West Indian immigrants to the United Kingdom, carrying 492 passengers in a voyage from Jamaica to London in 1948.

In ***A Woman of Destiny*** Manny, Velma's partner was from Jamaica, and his ex-girlfriend, Claudine, seems to have made the journey to join him in the UK relatively easy.

BORN IN ENGLAND

Darris, Darrin, Peter, 4 yr old Christopher and others from Joanne's holiday group were born in England of Grenadian migrant parents.

RETURN TO THE CARIBBEAN

Irene's body was returned to Grenada (for burial); Joanne went to accompany the body and to assist with Irene's burial. Mr. Mitchell spent 8 years, bought land in Grenada whilst in England and returned to farm the land.

FROM ENGLAND TO THE CARIBBEAN

Those who moved from England to the Caribbean are as follows: Four year old Christopher; Mr. McDonald, Scottish Estate/Plantation Owner; Mr. Jessup (***English Head Master***); Mr. Glover (***English music teacher***).

Additionally, Miss Gisbreth, who regularly visited Grenada during summer holidays, was **from Canada**.

"*Motherland*" Aspirations in the Diaspora

In ***A Woman of Destiny***, the **Prologue** begins with one of the novel's the main character; Irene, a Grenadian national, who migrated to England where she lived her adult life. Having died there, by request, her body was brought back to Grenada for burial. Her story is told in a **flash-back style**, where the reader is allowed to learn of Irene's story and that of other migrants, who also left the island for England. Immediately following this, the novel presents us with an influx of Grenadians leaving the island by boat bound for England.

We learn from characters, that going away to seek betterment abroad seems to be a widespread ambition among islanders. This is so for many reasons – the migrants had lived all their lives, to their point of travel, as British citizens and had all received an imposed British (colonial) education; governed by a system that was entirely British. Consequently, they were of the opinion that being British subjects, with an unswerving allegiance to Britain, they were truly going to the **"*Mother Country*."** For most of them the concept of Britain was that, **"England had a money-tree," (p.246)** meaning that it was a land of opportunities beyond measure, where they would be welcomed and treated as equal citizens of Britain and the Empire. Many of the early migrants, especially those who arrived in Britain in the late 1950's and early 1960's, such as Irene, Aunty Mary,

Calvin and others in ***A Woman of Destiny***, left before Grenada became independent from Britain in 1974.

In ***A Woman of Destiny***, we learnt that the Caribbean region had welcomed the Queen and Duke in a visit to the area, as a marked historical period that reinforced the allegiance and linkage to the British Crown. It is important to note that despite movements toward Self-government, and pending political independence from Britain, for these early migrants, the heart of their educational and psychological development, embodied a system of British upbringing that firmly etched in their psyches, an indelible identification with Britain.

The fact is, the system of British education in the Caribbean, meant that all education systems were ultimately managed from Britain (until the 1970's). In ***A Woman of Destiny***, Justin's dad shows off his colonial education when he talks nostalgically about British literary icons such as **Wordsworth, Blake and Shakespeare** and shows off his mastery by reciting a poem. He advocates engaging in and prioritizing the love of **"books" (p.50)** above all other forms of educational medium.

As a British colony, the population received an English curriculum, with resources and texts that were solely related to being British; (being British citizens in British colonial territories). Students' exam papers were marked in Britain and to all intents and purposes, many of the people's cultural practices imbued the British ways of life they were brought up with. It means that these migrants who arrived in Britain, qualified in various fields, had British exam certificates, which evidenced their qualifications but found they were not accepted for employment in England in the professions they were qualified and certified to do.

Prior to this, they were armed with such zeal, and enthusiasm to leave Grenada for Britain, that they left their children in the care of extended family members, while they migrated to England as economic migrants. It is because England had offered economic betterment – personally for individuals and especially for those who wanted to study; for whole families and also for the island as a whole. They had carried within them the full conviction that the Britain they had admired and were now living in is, and would always be their ***"Motherland."***

This is why in ***A Woman of Destiny***, Calvin wants to study to become a solicitor and during this historical period in England, it would have been a real possibility. However, his immediate family commitments took precedence and this frustrated him so much that he gave up his determination to succeed in his ambition. Calvin, like the majority of migrants, had to do jobs in various sectors of British society, i.e. catering, factory, transport, hospitals, and hotels, to name a few; in order to rebuild the Motherland after the war.

Byron, who had been an Estate Overseer in Grenada, was also defiant in refusing to do a menial job and instead choose unemployment. This defiance demonstrates their thought-processes, based on their colonial upbringing, and responses to the life-changing experiences that rejection in Britain had caused. The result is a complex web of behavioural responses and strategies for survival, in what they regarded as a ***harsh*** and ***violent*** reality for them and their families in England.

The reason is, not only were the adults experiencing the harshness of life in Britain but since the word "***violence***" can be used in a relative sense here; the children who were **branded** as ***"educationally sub-normal,"*** could also be seen as having experienced "***violence***" in the form of psychological damage exacted on the child/family's psyche. The reality of Caribbean children being branded as "***educationally sub-normal***" and being transported over long distances from home to schools that were referred to as "***Educationally Sub-Normal (ESN) schools,"*** is a form of psychological ***violence*** that many of the early parents grappled with.

In ***A Woman of Destiny***, the fear caused by this form of "***branding,***" seemed real to the migrants and this fear was articulated by Aunty Mary, as a caution to Irene, advising her to refuse offers of ESN schools for Joanne. Irene told Joanne one day, ***"I didn't spend all that money sending you to good schools back home to have you end up in some ENS school in England."…..Well ENS, ESN, call it whatever you want, you're not going there," (p.242).*** Added to this rejection were the daily experiences of racism Irene and the early migrants experienced at work, which created, what I would call, "**the double allegiance**" factor.

This means a complexity of holding on to the ***old*** psyche of colonial affectation and the ***new*** reality of having to adjust their previously held high expectations of Britain, to experiencing the reality of rejection, led them to hanker for "***back home***" – the Caribbean. It also led to a change in consciousness; from British to Caribbean allegiance. Such paths of convergence ultimately impacts on their behavioural responses to life as it affects them in Britain. What we witness among the Grenadian migrant is a confusion of emotional responses that can seem illogical at times. In ***A Woman of Destiny***, Irene, Calvin and Byron, could be seen as victims of this psychological complexity in ways that highlight the pathology of their behaviour.

Caribbean fruits

Mouthwatering Caribbean food

PROLOGUE SUMMARY & ANALYSIS

Summary

Joanne is in a Grenada cemetery, where she has returned to attend her mother's funeral; fulfilling a request that the body be returned **"home"** for burial. The theme of ***returning*** is ambivalent, as it's typical of what happens to Grenada/Caribbean migrants after years of sojourn in the metropolis, and eventually lacking in connectedness, vitality and folksiness with their roots. The funeral, we are told, is lackluster and is as customary as the Reverend Blackman's attire, pointing to a major difference that is confirmed later with the folks' response to Mark's funeral in **Chapter 4**. Even the ***"dying"*** sun seems to commiserate and there is a lack of participation by the women, as ***"no woman tied her belly, and no customary painful screams or appeals to the Divine"* (p.2)** were made. This relationship with the landscape is also symbolic of the relationship between the narrator and her mother – distant, philosophical, linked with unease, symbolized by the silk cotton tree's association with the soul of the undead.

A brief summary of the once ***"fallen comet;"*** introduces us to the sense of shame, lack of freedom, abandonment, village gossip, hurt, experienced by the 15 year old mother's teenage pregnancy and family's loss of reputation. Consequently, it presents the atmosphere that pervaded Joanne's entry into the world.

This **Prologue** is the **Introduction to the book or first Calypso song**, which the narrator reads/sings to us as a ***solo***, as she reflects on hers and her mother's life up to this point. Therefore, the beginning of the ***narrative or Calypso***, is ***a ballad of lament or blues*** about suffering, in which the symbolic landscape (which represents ***backing or a Calypso band***), is quiet; participating only as the rustling leaves which, ***"seem to be whispering their condolences," (p.6).*** But amidst the pages of the novel there is also a sense that the theme of ***"returning"*** rejuvenates, restores and re-directs. This is confirmed by Joanne when she says the landscape gives ***"promises of future peace," (p.6).*** Later in the Epilogue, convinced that all will be well she leaves this funeral spot to, ***"reconstruct my future," (p.309).*** Though the ending of the ***story/song*** is open-ended, as the ***music/narrative*** just seems to ***fade***; there is a sense of optimism for whatever path she decides to take in the future.

Analysis

Our narrator opens in Standard English, suggesting her current mode of expression, temporarily from her English environment (England), where she has spent the majority of her life to date. The very first sentence introduces the religious atmosphere that prepares us for the flashback of stories and a dominant aspect of the narrator's early life. The rest of the novel will go on to ***"sing"*** her recorded ***Calypsos/stories*** and lead the reader forwards and backwards in time, and in tune, to the ***songs/stories*** of the key players. The narrative voice which leads and introduces the main ***song/story*** is a part of this Grenadian community. It has witnessed many of the events in this landscape in **Part I**.

Furthermore, it is apparent, from the "I" narrator, and the impression of fictional realism, that the story is immediate and contemporary for the reader.

An image of the crowd or community here is ***muted***, and the prominence of ***"silence",*** is the sense of power that the natural landscape/the grave has, to "obliterate" the past and give way to new beginnings; like the story of Hurricane Janet as told in **Chapter 2**. It is also the final end to one ***quest/chapter/song***, as it establishes the beginning of another; but this time with a stronger sense of optimism and real independence.

Strategically, this cyclical movement of the main characters' lives is reminiscent of a kind of ***call-and-response*** technique of the Calypso, which is confirmed in the first **part/*call*** of a sentence tag; ***"As it was in the beginning,"* (p.1)** which **ends/*responds*** with the **Epilogue's** other half of the sentence, ***"so shall it be in the end,"* (p.304).** On another level, this structure can be seen as an imitation of the **"*Crick-crack*"** framework of the Caribbean storytelling tradition.

Joanne is privy to the whole ***song/narration***; having experienced or sung it before yet she, like her dead mother, can also be seen as a step removed from the landscape, the fact that they have been living outside of the natural Grenadian community/landscape. The narrator's speech is fluid, reminiscent of the Calypso tune that begins with a ***solo*** and moves to ***improvisation***, then later will include the support of the community, who are her ***musical/backing band***, (in both landscapes), in a ***narrative/Calypso song*** that has no set rules, as it ***'tells it [the story] like it is.'***

CHAPTER 1 – SUMMARY & ANALYSIS	
CHARACTERS	**RELATIONSHIPS**
Gran-gran – Catherine, Braveboy **Aunt Meena** **Catherine & Claudette** **Uncle Charles** **Irene** **Yvonne**	**Joanne's 70 yr old grandmother** **Joanne's Aunt** **Joanne's Cousins** **Joanne's uncle who died in England** **Joanne's mum** **Irene's daughter**
Lily – English woman **George - 65 yr old Trinidadian** **Ben 70yr old English man** **Joyce – English woman**	**Occupants in an Old People's Nursing Unit (Hospital in the UK)**
Mr. James – mixed race man **Ms Ivy - Grocer** **Septimus – Rum shop owner**	**Adult Villagers**
Jean **Gloria** **Dessima** **Daisy**	**Children of the Village**
Mr. Zephryn **Brother Charles** **Miss Mattis** **Miss Ruby** **Miss Letisha** **Brother Littleman**	**Villagers who are Joanne's neighbours**
Mr. McDonald (dead)	**Past plantation owner**

Events in this Chapter

1. Irene, the narrator's mother, is among patients in a Hospital Unit in England, where they seem to go unnoticed by the outside world.
2. The narrator's mind flashes back to when she was with her grandmother and we learn about her close relationship with her Grandmother, village life and the landscape in general.
3. Aunt Meena goes to town and in the conversation between the narrator and her grandmother we learn about the Grandmother's past experiences.
4. The landscape is described in detail and we see the villagers close relationship with one another.

5. The narrator has an interest in anything that's English and a main event in this Chapter is that her mother migrates from Grenada on a boat bound for England, as are many other people.

Chapter Summary

This Chapter opens up in a Hospital Unit in the UK, and introduces the elderly Irene, who's slightly deaf and disengaging. She has become silent, unaware of her surrounding and has no notion of time. However, Time has been personified to mock her, as revenge. The unsympathetic tone that describes her current situation suggests that this is a reciprocal exchange for what, we are told, she has inflicted on others in the past.

In contrast, the description of the other occupants in the ward is presented with a sense of humour; as we see the child-like adults, experiencing their second childhood. Ben is the naughty boy who is carefree and runs around and appears not to listen to anyone, whilst Joyce whose best friend had stolen her husband, is the stubbornly aggressive and selfish girl. George, on the other hand, is the mouthy comedian among them, with his tales of grandiloquence and fantastic imaginings of having met the Queen once.

Lily is the marionette-like, jolly singer, who smears lipstick over her face, appears to be stuck in time, clapping to her war-time memories with songs that are alive in her head. With this mixture of elderly people in a Hospital ward, the narrator's mum is relegated to spend her ***"last"*** days. Despite their many comic characteristics, there is a sense of abandonment about it. The difference, we are shown later, is that this ward is not peopled with folks or the community; it is a place where the narrator tells us, ***"They go unnoticed by the outside world,"* (p.11).**

In contrast, we are flashed backwards in time to the narrator's youth, where we meet her grandmother in the Caribbean setting. Gran-gran is presented as admirable, associated with bravery, as her name suggests, with a direct link to African ancestry; that of the Ashanti people. The narrator describes the village and the strategic proximity of the places it contains, which have meaning for the folks – a grocery store, a rum shop, a Post Office, a doctor's surgery, a Friendly Society Hall, a Seven Day Adventist church, and like the village chief, Mr. James' "big" house.

As narrator, Joanne is looking forward to a quiet time at home with her grandmother, because her Aunt Meena and cousins are going for a day's journey to town and the river, respectively. Joanne is left to prepare the usual mid-day bath for her grandmother and we learn about the healing powers of the natural herbs and their healing function on the body; all used by Joanne to prepare the grandmother's bath.

The narrator is excited that she is going to seize the moment to ask Gran-gran questions, as there were things her young inquisitive mind wanted to know about but was prevented from knowing via direct questioning. This is because the prevailing view was ***"children must be seen and not heard,"* (p.16)** because folks considered that they ***"asked too much questions,"* (p.16).** In contrast, Joanne tells us that her reasons for questioning was that she had become impatient with having to make sense of the cryptic sayings uttered by adults, and concluded that it was a widespread practice among other village families.

We learn that ***"life was the church and the church was our stage,"* (p.17)** meaning everything revolved around religious activities, which limited her opportunities for anything else. Doing chores, such as collecting water at 5.30am with other young girls, and following commands with threats of the repercussions for disobedience were real; punishment with a big stick. Joanne tells us of an occasion when she and her cousins were beaten by Aunt Meena with the ***"big stick"*** for disobeying her rules.

Village life is described in detailed narrative and in particular, the ***"noises"*** rising to a ***"crescendo,"*** provided by hens, donkeys, neighbours shouting, mixed in with competition from a variety of foreign religious and secular programmes; for the ***"loudest, clearest sound"*** that created a ***"carnival of radio programmes"* (p.19)** and a ***"village orchestra."*** There is a sense that with our without lyrics, music pervades the very atmosphere of the place. Before Aunt Meena leaves for the day's outing to town, she leaves strict instructions about chores to be performed by Joanne, in her absence. These are focused solely on caring for Gran-gran.

Descriptions of the landscape are in-depth; showing it to be a central character in the novel's plot. It is the backdrop where the ***backing-band*** (all the other characters), will join in and ***chorus*** or ***sing*** their individual ***Calypso ballads*.** A locus of affection and memory, village life and the villagers reflect the pulse of the village; is described with depictions of functionality and purpose. Whether good or bad, the narrator evades any censure, other than to introduce them as ***players in the band***. We learn of other functions of the natural landscape; its healing characteristics, via detailed knowledge of the local flora and their medicinal purposes. This is demonstrated in Joanne's preparation for her grandmother's bath and we see Joanne as instrumental in that process of healing and nurturing, as she tends to her grandmother.

In the time spent with her grandmother, Joanne listens to her family's history and in particular, a story of how her grandmother was raped by a past plantation owner. Among other histories of relics around the house, such as the mortar, an old mule's saddle and a grinding stone; we learn of the loss of Gran-gran's son in England. These problems appear occasionally to resurface, demonstrated by Gran-gran's visible, nervous, twitching and flickering eyelids that symbolize ***"trapped emotional pain located there,"* (p.26).** The narration describes how her grandmother coped with news of her son's loss and this foreshadows the loss of little Mark in the village later, in **Chapter 4**. As the novel develops, we see how at that time, Gran-gran's nervous twitching resurfaces by the painful memory that Mark's death evokes.

The young child is skilled in bathing and caring for her grandmother and their close relationship is one of discipleship or following elders and doing as she is told; apprenticeship or learning by doing, overhearing and being submissively obedient.

Preparations for Joanne's mother's departure from Grenada, is done swiftly, amidst a community participatory farewell. Details of the farewell are given to demonstrate the closeness, and unity of the supportive villagers, and an important aspect of the oral tradition in Grenada and the Caribbean region as a whole which is called ***Speechifying***; as Irene prepares to depart from Grenada. The farewell event presents a kind of half-formal but heart-rending emotional expressions which foreground the content of religion that is ingrained in the lives of the folks. The departing Irene, appears to be unmoved by the emotional demonstrations and, bent on following her plans to leave, wastes no time in bathing and preparing Joanne for the last time; the next day's journey to the harbour.

Joanne has an early interest in England via her English book, and has fantasies of being in that place; is established at this early stage in the novel. This is a foreshadowing of the narrator's continued fantasies throughout the novel, demonstrated by her role-playing with her best friend of life in England and her own journey to England, later in the novel.

Gran-gran did not go to the harbour to witness her daughter's departure but Joanne, who had accompanied the village folks, was left by her mother, on the bus that had brought them there. Joanne was sleeping on Miss Mattis' lap, while the departing adults busied themselves with official procedures for leaving the island. At that point, Joanne loses all physical contact with the mother and this is worsened by the fact that she is later unable to identify her mother's face amongst the waving crowds of leavers. The boat's horn boooed and signaled its farewell, while it ***"distanced"*** itself from Grenada's shores; symbolizing a distancing of the migrants with the Grenadian landscape. Finally, Joanne, who is emotionally traumatized with the enormity of the event, is brought back home to the village, where she will live with her Aunt Meena and Gran-gran.

Analysis

The relationship between the narrator and grandmother is a striking ***duo percussion*** set that relate lovingly to each other and their upbeat ***song/narrative*** is one which sustains Joanne's narrative and her character. Memories and associations lead the narrator to retell their relationship, as she highlights on intimate facets of their ***story/song.***

The details of their relationship and the introduction of Aunt Meena project a recurring ***trio***; whose ***songs/stories*** provide the essence of life as lived in the Grenadian landscape. Aunt Meena, most of the times, has a strong lead in the ***trio*, ** as she instructs, guides, and punishes with a big stick. This is presented with her own brand of nurturing, which portrays her as a ***lead singer in this 3 piece band***. Her perfunctory exchanges with Joanne is a kind of ***call-and-response*, ** as she instructs the young narrator of jobs that need doing in her absence; failing which there will be physical punishment, ***"if you can't hear you must feel"* (p.19).**

There is a sense that physical punishment pervades the landscape, and the public beating which the girls get on the street by Aunt Meena, is a kind of foreshadowing of the corporal punishment the narrator and her friend receive publicly, in front of 500 pupils at school; as well as the vicious fight between two women - Jean and Dessima - publicly on the streets.

The language used to describe Aunt Meena foreshadows that of Joanne's absent mother. Her style of caring is projected as 'love' which is held in check via reprimands, censure, threats, physical punishments, since we are told, ***"you did not cross her path, no, not at all!"* (p.19).** As the narrator's story is told, she digresses to explore the folksiness of the secondary characters and the part played by the villagers as a whole, in helping to create that **"*woman of destiny*."**

The villagers are presented as members of the narrator's ***backing band*** and we see their individual ***solos*** presented as a kind of ***call-and-response****;* as they briefly introduce each other on entering the bus to the town. These upbeat ***solos*** are presented before the slower ***rhythm*** of the narrator and grandmother's ***solo*,** as they are left to discuss a sociological phenomena or historical truth. This is presented in the Grenadian vernacular to give primacy to the lives as it's led by the characters in the landscape. At one point, the ten year old Joanne is surprised when her grandmother responds to the questions she poses. The unexpected responses from her grandmother appear to shift cultural protocol, when she is told of the grandmother's rape in the distant past, by Mr. McDonald, the plantation owner. This again reinforces the image of violence against the person, in this case, motivated by the ***powerful*** over the ***powerless***.

Joanne's questions to her grandmother during their conversation whilst alone in the house seem to mimic the ***call-and-response*** structure of the Calypso. Joanne questions and her grandmother answers; demonstrates how folk wisdom is passed on - via oral transmission, as is also done in a Calypso rendition. In this case, Gran-gran does it as a form of ***verbal caution and to inspire good sense*** in Joanne; evidencing another characteristic of the Calypso.

The ***rhythm*** of language in Gran-gran's shocking tale is reflective of the all-inclusiveness of subject matters in song; as far as Calypsonians are concerned. Characteristically, the Calypsonian's duty is to tell all, or **"*like it is*"** (as Gran-gran did). Musically, this may come as an ***unexpected improvisation***, showing how violence is dramatised in the internal world of a key character and also resonates externally, in the historical world of Slavery/Plantation days.

In ***telling it like it is*,** Gran-gran is able to teach the young narrator how to make cocoa, and relate the history of their family. Gran-gran **"*did not know her father*,"(p.19)** nor does the young narrator, and Gran-gran's role here is to help the young girl avoid the pitfalls and pain she has experienced; which at times seem to resurface under extreme emotional pressure. Therefore, what may appear superficially, to be shocking tactics of relating the details of adverse events (such as the rape), they are done culturally to actually teach the young girl; in other words, to prevent recurrences of learning by your mistakes. By the same token, when details are not relevant for the young child's ears, we see the village women's deliberate, exclusionary tactics; they break into the **French Creole** vernacular.

The 70year old Gran-gran shares in leading the narrator's ***Calypso/narrative*** and as head matriarchy, she represents the wisdom of the folk; appearing to span two generations, having experienced some aspects of the island's French and English colonial dominance. It is the reason why the majority of her language and that of the older villagers, is spoken as *patois* (pronounced ***patwa***) or **French Creole**. Her ***solo/narrative*** is presented as a history of the folk from her perspective and when she talks, her conversations are not extraneous, but we are told she is referred to as an impartial referee, who has the unquestionable authority to pass ***"judgment."***

She is a silent sufferer, having lost her son in England under questionable circumstances, did not know her father, was brutally raped by her **"master"** and there is no information about her own personal family i.e. husband. However, her character is symbolic of the witnessing mortar and pestle; the grinding stone and saddle, whose presence is effectively one of ***"reminding."*** In her elderly matriarchal role, she is the transmitter of cultural wisdom and protector of the younger women of the village; as was demonstrated in the episode with the *"African priest"* (**Chapter 3**).

We are shown the first interaction between the narrator and her mother (Irene), only as she prepares to leave the island. However, this brief interlude is done to show the ceremonious role that is played out between the two. The quick splashing and rubbing, ***quickens the rhythm of the song*** and shows there's little time for emotional tenderness; its performed as a quick duty with short, sharp instructions that signify a kind of relationship where Irene must not show deep emotions. The concern shown for the child is that she obeys her elders; get a good education by ***"learning in school"* (p.28)** and a promise of being sent for to join her in England.

Irene's solo is a staccato rhythm, characterized by abruptly disconnected elements. However, it's the first time we are told of the mother's emotional connection with the narrator. This is done in her parting comments, after the symbolic washing, prior to her expressed wish for Joanne to ***"have a destiny."*** The meaning of the word ***"destiny"*** for Joanne's mother and later for the village folks is translated as expecting ***something good, fortunate and extraordinary to happen to Joanne that characterizes her future success***. Their wider frame of reference is that Joanne's success will ultimately be adopted as their own personal successes too. Here, the washing of the child, ***"the last quick care,"* (p.29)** though performed as a **"*duty*,"** could symbolize a form of purification/cleansing, in preparation for the child's eventual claim to her ***destiny*.**

Irene seems to project a tough exterior, adamant, and whose love is described as **"*momentarily*"** and who **did not weaken emotionally** at her farewell event. In fact, it was no surprise that she had left the sleeping child on the bus, as she made her way to the waiting ship, bound for England. The narrator is emotionally distraught, when she wakes to find the mother gone, and cannot identify her face in ***"the sea of smiling faces,"* (p.32)** waving to the Grenadians being left behind. Joanne waves but her mother is engulfed by the crowd of travellers migrating to England. At this point, the gap between Joanne and her mother widens, as she is unable to single her out in a crowd. The narration too, draws attention to the movement of the ship ***"as it distanced itself"* (p.33)** from Grenada,

***"further and further it moved away,"* (p.33)** signifying the beginning of distance, when **memory** will begin to arrogate its authority over what's no longer seen. The passengers for England had travelled on the bus to the harbour, in the early hours of the morning. On reaching the harbour, all the passengers alighted but the sleeping Joanne was left to rest on Miss Mattis' lap.

The final passages in this Chapter present a vivid documentary of expectant Grenadians' last farewell, in what seems like curtains coming down, as if on a stage. The suggestion here is that these migrating islanders seem to be in a performance (i.e. as their duty, acting, or masked); as they departure is symbolic of taking a bow on stage. Perhaps in further Acts, the curtains would rise again; at another scene and at some other time. At this point, there is a sense that the narration, like Calypso music, appears to rise to a **"*crescendo,*"** generated by the ***"laughter, talking, tooting of horns which caused instant confusion in this early morning carnival,*" (p.32)** then fades ***"slowly,"*** as the ***narration/song*** comes to an end.

This scene foreshadows the return of the corpse to Grenada, in its final curtain call, in the **Epilogue** and confirms that, ***"as it was in the beginning, so shall it be in the end."* (p304).** They take their leave of Grenada's soil, but at some point they return. Interestingly, the structure of the novel is that it does come full circle, and the final section or **Epilogue** is also the place (**Prologue**), where the novel initially began. This can be a reminder of the timelessness and supremacy of nature, of how our natural world tolerates our troubled lives and ultimately bears witness to the inevitability of our natural demise.

CHAPTER 2 – SUMMARY & ANALYSIS

CHARACTERS	RELATIONSHIPS
Gran-gran **Aunt Meena** **Joanne**	**Joanne's 70 yr old Grandmother** **Joanne's Aunt** **The Narrator**
Justin **Justin's dad** **Emma** **Phyllis**	**Emma's cousin** **Mr. Egbert Thomas** **Joanne's best friend** **Emma's sister**
Sukram Cheema **Lola** **Itran** **Mr. Zephryn** **Mr. Mitchell** **Miss Joseph** **Miss Flora** **Boysie** **Jean** **Letisha** **Miss Cleothilda** **Cousin Seeviny** **Charlie** **Mr. & Mrs. Kent** **Daisy & Jassinta**	**40 yr old villager** **Sukram's wife** **Sukram's best friend** **Rum shop owner** **Returned migrant, landowner** **Villager, Joanne's Godmother (*Nenen*)** **Villager whose husband, Boysie, died** **Miss Flora's husband** **A villager, looking after Letisha, her sister's child** **Jean's neice** **Gran-gran's neighbour** **A villager, Joanne's relative** **Justin's dad drinking pal** **Past White land owners** **Village children, listening to the storytelling**

Events in this Chapter

1. Joanne a model obedient child, shown in the child's active care of her grandmother.
2. Joanne returns to the subject of the Grenadian migrants, bound for England and we learn what Justin, a childhood friend, thinks of the travellers' predicament.
3. Justin compares their treatment to that of prisoners on board the ship to England.
4. Joanne narrates the gruesome murder of Itran by Sukram, a ***"crazy Indian man,"* (p.36).** The 40 year old Sukram had become insane and harpooned Itran, his best *friend*, who cheated on him with his wife.
5. Having drowned his sorrows with rum until he was quite drunk and clearly mad; Sukram parades the village street, holding his friend's severed head and saying that he had ***"caught a big fish,"* (p.36).**
6. Joanne's daily act of reading from a religious ***"Words of Comfort"*** book to her grandmother is a multifunction act that simultaneously helps to guide Joanne, create a bond between her and Gran-gran and develop her reading skill.

7. Gran-gran and Miss Joseph strike up a conversation which is partly expressed in the Grenada **Creole French** they give each other the ***"low down."***
8. Joanne finishes her chores and takes the opportunity, while her grandmother is asleep, to find her best friend Emma. She takes a short-cut through a trace which has a boundary with Mr. Mitchell; a kind, religious, villager who had migrated to England but has returned to live in Grenada.
9. Joanne meets Justin, Emma's 12 year old cousin in the trace and he is playful with her. Joanne's approaching puberty is shown in exchanges between her and Justin.
10. Joanne speaks openly and innocently about her developing breast size, her interest in her bodily changes, talks with her friends about their menstrual cycles, wearing childish dresses with bands tied at the back, and the adults' refusal to straighten the girls' hair.
11. Aunt Meena narrates her own reasons for the staunch attitude she adopts in her refusal to let Joanne participate in activities outside the village e.g. local concerts, Tivoli Harvest Festival, and Carnival.
12. In contrast to the treatment of girls, we are shown for the first time, how Justin, their male counterpart, is treated and the role of the men in a rum shop.
13. Justin's dad boasts about past skills, (e.g. showing off his colonial education, in his ability to recite the poetry of **Wordsworth, Blake and Shakespeare.**
14. He is very vocal in his derision of emerging new cultural trends such as Rastafarianism, the idea of '***going back to Africa,***' and ***reggae music,* (p.48)** compared to the Calypso.
15. As with the villager's stated wish for Joanne to become a ***woman of destiny***, Justin's dad also expects his son to excel and become a lawyer, so that he too can adopt the boy's ***success/destiny*** as his own.
16. When Joanne reaches Emma's house, the girls play out their fantasies and we see them imitating an English life-style they imagine, based on their perceptions of bourgeois lifestyle.
17. The girls' vision of pretending to be pregnant or to live in England is role-played and this behaviour seems to sustain their interest throughout **Part I**; until their expected departures from Grenada, to join their 'absent' parents in England.
18. With a flashback, we are given details by master story-tellers; Aunt Meena and Gran-gran. The village children sit in the moonlight, listening to the experiences of the two women and others who had experienced **Hurricane Janet in 1955**.

Chapter Summary

In the previous Chapter, the novel had set the scene for the relationship between Joanne and Gran-gran and this relationship is lovingly portrayed by the narration in this Chapter. ***Attila the Hun's*** (Raymond Quevedo) Calypso, tagged at the beginning of the Chapter, suggests the, ***"bewitching, captivating, fascinating, throbbing and absorbing nature of the West Indian rhythm,"* (p.34).** There is double entendre here; the pun on 'West Indian rhythm' could suggest that the folks' rhythm of life in the landscape, which exemplifies all of the above descriptions, and at the same time, it portrays characteristics of the tone, tempo and pulse of the ***Calypso song/narration*.** Joanne is presented at the beginning of this Chapter as a model obedient child, shown in the child's active care of her grandmother. This includes the ritual bath, dressing, combing her ***"dougla"*** hair and their tête-à-tête during discussions about the recent departure of Irene from Grenada.

Joanne returns to the subject of the Grenadian migrants, bound for England and we learn what Justin, a childhood friend, thinks of the travellers' predicament. He compares their treatment to that of prisoners on board the ship to England. This information is given briefly, as a thought that Joanne's remembers during her conversation with Gran-gran. Justin is typical of the older men, whose mannerisms he imitates. He appears to be full of information, which Joanne and the children listen to.

This engaging image of quietude and peacefulness is suggestive of a ***slower paced Calypso*** sung by a ***duo percussionist,*** who is at one with themselves and the world. That harmony, like their peace and apparent comfort, is maintained in the ***narration/song***, until it is disturbed by Joanne's memory recall of when Justin had broken the news of a shocking event in the village. She remembers the gruesome murder of Itran by Sukram, a ***"crazy Indian man."*** The 40 year old Sukram had become insane and harpooned Itran, his best *friend*, who cheated on him with his wife.

The ***narrative/song*** flashes back to the two men's relationship up to this point of horror. Sukram had refused to believe the gossips about his wife's infidelity until he caught them red-handed and consequently took the only action his *insane* mind drove to take. Having drowned his sorrows with rum until he was quite drunk and seemingly mad; Sukram parades the village street, holding his friend's severed head and saying that he had ***"caught a big fish;"*** much to the horror of the villagers. Lola, who is blamed and derided by the villagers, leaves Sukram and flees with their three children to St. David, another parish, to live with her sister.

The narration skips forward to the present, where Joanne and her Grandmother are comfortable, and where peace reigns. Joanne plaits Gran-gran's hair, puts on her shawl, and then performs her daily act of reading from a religious ***"Words of Comfort"*** book to her grandmother. Reading has multifunction – simultaneously, it helps to guide Joanne, to create a bond between her and Gran-gran and to develop her reading skill.

Gran-gran sits in the verandah, where she observes and communicates with Miss Cleothilda, a neighbour; as well as passers-by and workers going to and from work. Miss Joseph, a land worker, has been doing the same physical work as the men folk. Gran-gran and Miss Joseph strike up a conversation which is partly expressed in the Grenada Creole French. The women exchange local information, by giving each other the ***low-down*** or local gossip. Joanne appears with drinking water for Miss Joseph, who gives them some of the ground provisions; she collected from her job to Gran-gran before leaving.

Gran-gran then falls asleep during Joanne's reading of her ***Words of Comfort*** book. Gran-gran's book is a recurring motif throughout the novel, (especially in the relationship between Gran-gran and Joanne). Joanne finishes her chores and takes the opportunity, while her grandmother is asleep, to find her best friend Emma. She takes a short-cut through a trace which has a boundary with Mr. Mitchell; a kind, religious, villager who had migrated to England but has returned to live in Grenada.

Joanne meets Justin, Emma's 12 year old cousin in the trace and he is playful with her. Joanne's approaching puberty is shown in the exchanges between her and Justin. He is a cocky, precocious boy, who Joanne is warned she must keep at bay; despite her feelings of loneliness as a child.

The narrator tells us how Justin's interest in her feels: ***"it sent ripples and bubbles of excitement inside my body and I stifled the tingling feeling inside me,"* (p.50).** Girls are told ***"not to run around with boys"*** and Joanne talks of the cultural discipline instilled in them regarding boys in general; a situation she says that causes a ***"mixture of excitement and fear,"* (p.50).** Joanne speaks openly and innocently about her developing breast size, her interest in her bodily changes, talks with her friends about their menstruation cycles, wearing childish dresses with bands tied at the back, and the adults' refusal to straighten a girl's hair. This is associated with visible signs of maturity which must not be publicized to the male population.

The narration flashes to an occasion in the past, to portray Aunt Meena's over-protectiveness of Joanne. In fact, Aunt Meena narrates her own reasons for the staunch attitude she adopts in her refusal to let Joanne participate in activities outside the village e.g. school concerts, Tivoli Harvest Festival, and Carnival. We learn later that her fears are not unfounded, as Joanne and Emma imitate pregnant women in their childish role-playing; suggestive of something that is admired by the young girls!

In contrast to the treatment of girls, we are shown for the first time, how Justin, their male counterpart, is treated and the role of the men in a rum shop. However, unlike the women, the men appear stultified. Justin's dad boasts about past skills, (e.g. showing off his colonial education, in his ability to recite the poetry of **Wordsworth, Blake and Shakespeare**. His boasts include wearing leather shoes, as opposed to Washicon (cheap rubbery plimsols); wearing clean clothes, smelling sweet, and looking good with a part in his hair and a fine handwriting style.

Again, we see his preference for the book-form; as Justin's dad shows off his knowledge of Standard English terms – ***"etymology, phonology, syntax, and prosody"*** which, at the same time, are presented as, ***"confusion in his head,"* (p.49).** He is very vocal in his derision of emerging new cultural trends such as Rastafarianism, the idea of '***going back to Africa***,' and ***reggae music***, compared to the ***Calypso* (p.48)**.

Justin imitates men-talk, their mannerisms and unlike the girls, is given ***unfettered freedom.*** As with the villager's stated wish for Joanne to become a ***Woman of Destiny***, Justin's dad also expects his son to excel and become a lawyer, so that he too can adopt the boy's ***success/destiny*** as his own. Appearing to be 'stuck' in his time of life, this dad laments his apparent failed ambitions; especially when he is drunk, and publicly advises his son to break with the tradition of working on the land.

Justin's dad talks about working on the land which he sees as a sign of regression. The result of this type of labour, he thinks, is that you become a ***"rum-head and vagabond,"* (p.49).** Instead, he advocates reading books, ***"learning to read and spell good,"* (p.49)** as a sign of educational and social advancement. Therefore, in his drunken stupor outside the rum shop, he promptly instructs his son to go home to ***"get out you books,"* (p.).** Justin's dad's contemporaries, like Cleveland, have moved on and has become a lawyer in America; a success he equates with achieving the kind of ***"destiny,"*** he projects for Justin.

When Joanne reaches Emma's house, the girls play out their fantasies and we see them imitating an ***imagined*** English life-style, based on their perceptions of typical bourgeois lifestyle. The girls' vision of pretending to be pregnant or to live in England is role-played and this behaviour seems to sustain their interest throughout **Part I**; until their expected departures from Grenada, to join their 'absent' parents in England.

Joanne is forced to leave Emma's house, due to the threat of rain and rolling thunder. Luckily, she rushes home in time to save Gran-gran's clothes from becoming soaked from a downpour, and avoids possible interrogation from Aunt Meena for her absence from the home.

Safely inside, she witnesses the heavy downpour and this reminds her of stories she has heard about **Hurricane Janet**. With a flashback, we are given details by master story-tellers; Aunt Meena and Gran-gran. The village children sit in the moonlight, listening to the experiences of the two women and others who had experienced **Hurricane Janet in 1955**. In this story, we are also told about two villagers, Cosmos and his father whose story, like the Brer Anancy, Compere Tigg and Compere Zaen traditional stories, create screams of laughter from the listeners. But Gran-gran, who regards the **Janet story** as something quite serious, does not approve of the children's laughter.

Analysis

The narration in the opening paragraphs of this Chapter, presents the landscape as the background/***backing band***, where we will see the performances of the various characters/***singers***. In turn, they weave in and out of the ***Calypso composition***, either as ***solos, duets and group percussionists***. The Chapter narrates like a ***Calypso medley***, as we see a number of ***song-formations*** which makes up this Chapter.

The ***Calypso medley*** ranges from the *solidifying a relationship between Joanne and her grandmother - talk of the migrants bound for England - Sukram gruesome murder - Gran-gran tête-à-tête, giving the lowdown with her neighbour - gossip of the pregnant girl and her near mishap; Boysie's death; the slow pace of the consultation with the Words of Comfort book - Mr. Mitchelle's return to Grenada from England - the emerging 'puppy love' between Joanne and Justin - Justin's father's lament of failed ambitions and his take on newly emerging cultural trends, as well as his advice regarding working on the land - the dilemma and struggles of families caring for their migrant relatives children - Carnival blues and the different perspectives on the tradition - Joanne and Emma's role- playing "big women" - the storytelling of Cosmos and the infamous*

Hurricane Janet. Some of these ***songs*** will continue in other Chapters to join other ***medleys***, on different occasions, as they form the collective ***rhythm*** and ***beat*** of the novel. As with **Chapter 1**, the narrator again brings us back to the local remedies found in the herbs and medicinal bush found in the locality; highlighting their uses which the older women conclude is better than ***"any doctor medicine,"* (p.41).** We are shown a difference in folk perspective with the younger generation, who we are told, disregard the value of the ***'bush medicine,'*** in preference for the modern, manufactured medicines. Interestingly, the women talk of 'bush medicine' but include the use of ***thermogene*;** which is a manufactured compound. Inadvertently, this inclusion alludes to the benefit of a combination of *old* and *modern* medicine; though the women appear to be unaware of this.

This is reflective of the fusion of generic forms **(*book or literary* vs. *the voice or oral*);** a point that is intimated by Justin's dad and his drinking partners. In fact, Justin's dad is quite implicit in his view of the power of the book, versus doing physical labour on the land as an occupation. These views are perhaps symbolic of a dominant motif in the book, Gran-gran's insistence on Joanne reading to her daily from their, ***"Words of Comfort"*** book.

The constant engagement with the book-form provides the antithesis of the orally transmitted tradition and culture, among the women. This could be suggestive of the transformation from oral to literary tradition or a combination of both; intertwined to form the tapestry that will present the generic fusion linking Joanne to her ***destiny***.

The narrative of Gran-gran and Miss Mitchell's ***duo,*** is a gossiping conversation that resembles a ***call-and-response*** in their exchange; with subjects which ranges from Boysie's death, Letisha's pregnancy and her Aunt's shocking displeasure with the threat of physical beating of the pregnant girl. The women's tête-à-tête deliberately slips into Grenada **French Creole**, to exclude Joanne's understanding of what they are discussing. However, as a child who spends time overhearing conversations, Joanne is able to silently tap into the collective psyche of the elderly folks as a form of cultural education.

Like the overhearing Joanne, Justin is an observer of the male perspective. We are presented with Justin's imagery of the migrating folks, which is quite significant. This is because the language he uses to describe the passengers situation, is reflective of Trans-Atlantic slave-ships from West Africa, transporting slaves to the Caribbean via British ports like London, Liverpool and Bristol; when they carried goods and exchanged them for people to work on Caribbean plantations.

Justin is only 12 years old, but in adopting the mannerisms and talk of the men in the village rum shop, he describes the migrants' 21-day journey as follows: ***"You don't come out, you eat, shit and sleep in the same place and nobody cares if you sick or die.* (p.52). *Cooped up like a caged animal!"* (p.39)** The image is symbolic of a kind of ***'return journey'*** of the Middle passage being undertaken. Justin's dad intimated that there is also talk of ***"going back to Africa,"* (p.48).**

This theme of ***"returning"*** also shows that not all migrant journeys are futile because the cyclical journey had worked out well for Mr. Mitchell. His 7 years stay in England had enabled him to buy 8 acres of land; which his brother had maintained for him while in England and which they now cultivate successfully. Therefore, whether physically or as a form of raising consciousness, there is suggestion of a kind of ***cyclical journey*** taking place among characters.

The theme of ***innocence*** is presented and this is shown as the village children puzzle out their development; dominated by their adults' cryptic information about what to do during their adolescence. Adults shroud the menstruating phenomenon in parables, with a flurry of unexplained ***do's*** and ***don'ts*** – such as, not taking part in their school's extra-curricular activities or local events, never sleeping in someone else's house, and deliberately forcing a kind of child-like appearance on the developing girls; in order to ward off attention from the males. This retrogressive attitude symbolises a kind of deliberate **blinding or controlled ignorance,** caused by a desperate need to protect the girls. It is the women's method of dealing with the girls' **approaching signs of womanhood**.

Aunt Meena's objection, (like other family caring for young children in their parent's absence); is motivated by fear that things might go wrong e.g. pregnancy; especially as she is responsible for an absentee, migrant-relative's child. The fear is of reprehension from relatives in England and also fear and competition among villagers, who operate in society also as surrogate 'Carers;' by virtue of their cultural and traditional practice. ***"What your mother go say, all the way in England, if anything happen,"* (p.52).**

Therefore, from the perspective of a child, 'England' is also seen as something that causes retardation or stultifies growth. Joanne says that as a result, she became a ***"listener"*** and not a ***"talker,"*** (e.g. 15 yr old Phyllis, 10 yr old Emma, and 12 yr old Justin); because by comparison, the other children were given a degree of freedom to learn outside the confines of their homes; not ***"cooped up with the least to offer in a conversation,"* (p.52).** Those occasions of Aunt Meena's intransigence show a difference in styles of upbringing between Gran-gran and Aunt Meena; ultimately it's Aunt Meena who has the final say.

This is significant, because the paradox presented in wanting Joanne to be a '*future*' ***'woman of destiny'*** does not square with refusal to let her participate in her '*present*' burgeoning, cultural interests and opportunities to develop. However, we learn that Joanne's interest in Carnival developed, despite objections by her religious Gran-gran and Aunt Meena's attempt to stifle it. They see carnival as ***"the work of the devil,"* (p.53).** It would seem that such objections seem to evoke defiance (for good or bad); as demonstrated by not only Joanne, but also the priest who joined in the carnival festivities; as is recorded in a Calypso.

During the storytelling session, Gran-gran and Aunt Meena give first-hand information of their own personal suffering during **Hurricane Janet's** destruction and the children laugh at the humour created by Cosmos and his father's predicament during the hurricane. This sub-text of this story shows that nature/the landscape can be totally destructive, as opposed to its healing qualities presented at the start of the novel. It suggests that nothing can be taken at face value. The storytellers now adopt a ***'grinning mask,'* (p.58)** as they use a tragedy to provide 'entertainment' to the children.

The **Hurricane Janet** story is told as a historical account and shared experience, which cemented lives together. However, Gran-gran is not amused by the children's comical response to the historic devastation; she leaves the group with a parable, ***"teet doh always laughs good tings,"* (p.66).** This means from her perspective, it's not really a laughing matter. There is a suggestion that the children's modern response to the **Janet** story does not square with the enormity of the situation the women had experienced; hence laughter is an inappropriate response to their ***"watery tale."***

There is an emergent theme of ***perspectives*** here, as the children's focus is on the ***comedy*** evoked in Cosmos and his dad's response to the hurricane ***drama;*** whereas Gran-gran's focus is the ***near-death experience,*** as a whole.

The ***music***, like the characters' ***improvisation***, changes when considered from different vantage points. The shifting of focus is also reflected in individual character's different attitude towards carnival and inadvertently, Calypso music. Joanne's deeply religious family sees it as ***"the work of the devil,"* (p.53).** Joanne questions their logic because despite their objection, she sees it as part of everyone's ***"cultural tradition."*** Justin's dad too, has a definite preference for Calypso, as opposed to the emerging popularity of reggae. The inclusion of the carnival-participating priest's story, suggest that at times, culture takes precedence over the currency of religious views; thus it confirms Joanne's own defiant stance on the carnival.

CHAPTER 3 – SUMMARY & ANALYSIS	
CHARACTERS	**RELATIONSHIPS**
Joanne **Gran-gran** **Aunt Meena** **Charles**	**Narrator** **Joanne's 70 yr old Grandmother** **Joanne's Aunt** **Joanne's uncle**
Justin's dad **Emma** **Jessica** **Egbert** **Mr. Jessup** **Dr. Japal**	**Mr. Egbert Thomas** **Joanne's best friend** **Justin dad's wife** **Jessica's husband** **Headmaster of the local school** **The local doctor**
Reverend Blackman **Miss Jomen, Mother Sayee, Mother Mitchell, Brother Little, Brother Benjamin, Brother Raphael,** **The 'African' Priest**	**Village priest of the Baptist Church** **Members of the congregation at the Baptist Church** **An imposter**

Events in this Chapter

1. The Queen and the Duke's visit to the Caribbean region.
2. Children are drilled to near-perfection in the hot sun by Mr. Jessup, the local school Headmaster in readiness for the Royal welcome.
3. Calypsonians sing about the event.
4. There is a free competition for anyone to compose Grenada's National Anthem
5. The lyrics and style of **Men of Harlech** is Joanne's example.
6. Egbert Thomas, Justin's dad, mocks and jeers Joanne and her attempts. He is psychologically on a revenge trail, full of *"his pangs of regrets and reproaches,"* (p.77).
7. An *"African priest"* came to their village, after many talks of independence and Grenada's new national anthem. The 'priest' is accepted uncritically, when he suggests he could teach the children their *"African roots."* He was spoilt like a chief and was offered the villager's best.
8. The 'priest' makes sexual advances towards the girls and sexually fondles them.
9. Gran-gran and Aunt Meena are unaware of this – instead they guess Joanne's reaction is from being unwell from eating too many mangoes, so they give her a castor oil as a laxative.
10. Discovery that the *"African priest"* was a fraudster – not a priest and not African.

Chapter Summary

Joanne tells us that about the Queen and the Duke's visit to the region, when many islanders took part in the celebrations for the Royal visit; waving Union Jacks and enjoying the free cakes and sweet drinks given as treats. Schools were hives of activities, as children were drilled to near-perfection in the hot sun by Mr. Jessup, the local school Headmaster, in readiness for the Royal welcome. An ex-army General, Mr. Jessup was their 'live' symbol of colonization. Calypsonians sang about the event and helped to influence people's thought about the merriment being made for the occasion.

Despite the focus on the visitors, in the background there is also preparation for the island's impending celebration of independence. The coming event offers a free competition to anyone who wants to take part and compose the island's own National Anthem. Joanne attempts to take part and thinks of styling her own contribution like the kind of rousing, fervent songs she learnt at school.

Joanne gives an example of one song, +**Men of Harlech,** whose meaning seems puzzling with irrelevant content. The lyrics of this particular song she says was unrelated to their environment. Quizzing the adults around her showed they also knew little about the meaning or content, other than some vague linkages with the song being sung when West Indian men were going off to help Britain during World War II.

While Joanne is alone trying to compose her national anthem, Justin's dad (Egbert Thomas), comes up to her and mocks her, by jeering at her attempts. He puts her ability down, with cruel words that psychologically shock her into moments of low self-esteem. As someone who seems to be frustrated with not having achieved his ambitions, Justin's dad seems to be on a revenge trail, spending his time bragging about what he used to be able to do. We learn that he was once popular, had visions of migrating to America, like his brother and school friend. He loves his colonial education, especially his knowledge of English.

However, life turned sour for him as he was forced to marry Jessica, a local girl, who fell pregnant for him. She is from a bourgeois family whose father feels he is unsuitable for his daughter and brands him ***"a worthless rum-head, saga boy,"* (p.77).** Justin's dad's wife had died, leaving him to bring up his children - Jessica and Justin. He is often sorrowful, spends a good deal of time in the local rum-shop, drinking rum, to help him deal with, ***"his pangs of regrets and reproaches,"* (p.77).**

Two years after this incident, an ***"African priest"*** comes to the village, following talks of independence and Grenada's new National Anthem. The ***'priest'*** who is accepted uncritically, suggests he teaches the children their ***'African roots.'*** He is welcomed into the local St. Johns Baptist church and works alongside Reverend Blackman, the local priest. Gran-gran snatches up every opportunity of learning about the children's ***'African roots'*** for Joanne to excel, by letting her attend all sessions with the priest.

The church members make special efforts to accommodate and embrace the 'priest' and prayer is said enthusiastically, showing their gratitude for the 'African priest'. The priest responds with ***"invoking the African ancestral gods"*** in ***"an unknown language,"*** **(p.87).** We also learn that ***"he was spoilt like a chief being offered the villager's best"*** **(p.),** which included ***"Big succulent chunks of fried fish covered under new table cloths were brought to him; thick fried coo-coo pieces with ochras, roasted breadfruit, succulent avocado pears, freshly pounded coco and stout milk-drink with eggs and spice,*** **(p89).** Therefore, it is surprising when we learn later that, despite their extra special hospitality; the 'priest' had been interfering with the girls by sexually fondling them.

Joanne reacts to this by making excuses not to go to the priest's sessions, instead of telling her grandmother and Aunt Meena the truth. The women guess that she is unwell and gives her castor oil, which is a laxative; believing her to be suffering from eating too many fruits. Joanne takes the punishment, despite knowing it was not the kind of '***purge***' she needed. All the girls agonize over their predicament but refuse to tell their parents/guardians, for fear of how this information would be acted on.

However, Gran-gran suspects that things are amiss as she is puzzled by Joanne's behaviour; she monitors the girl's movement. She perceives that a problem exists which involves the 'African priest'. She uses her experience and skills and is able to psychologically challenge 'the priest' by her actions. At the same time, Justin enlightens Joanne and his cousin Emma, about information he hears, that the 'African priest' was a *fraudster – he was not a priest and he was not African!* After a meeting between Gran-gran and the elders of the village, the 'priest' is hastily dispatched from the village.

Analysis

In this Chapter, we are shown a change in consciousness among the folk, with various exits and entrances of individuals who represent the dying embers of colonialism: (the Queen and the Duke's visit), a craving for change, as seen in the ***"talk of independence,"*** **(p.68)** as well as the uncritical acceptance of an ***"African"*** priest, who has come to raise the black consciousness of the folks by looking at African culture as an alternative to colonialism. In their thirst for knowledge with the introduction of Africa as the ***"Motherland",*** we see how this made them vulnerable and exposed the children to the risk of real danger. (See more details in: *Men and Destiny – The African Priest*).

This signals several levels of changes in the island; some of which had already been intimated by Justin's dad, in the previous Chapter. Musically, the narrator presents her anthem competition in a style which is characteristic of the styles of competition for the ***"Calypso Monarch"*** of the year. Annually, each Calypsonian usually competes for the ***calypso crown,*** which would usually be determined by the best rendition and execution of a Calypso composition. Symbolically, the contesting Calypsos here could be regarded as those represented by ***colonialism, Africanism and Independence.***

Whether with or without lyrics, the essence of the issues taking place is both from a cultural and socio-political level. These are the different changes taking place in society;

but also can be seen here as the different musical styles and sentiments expressed by the Calypsonian as the *"people's newspaper."*

However, while one era is hastily coming to an end, and new ideals are being taken on board, there are questions in-between, which the young narrator puzzles over: unclear historical facts and their meaning and their relevance to her 'young' world. This is portrayed in discussions about West Indian soldiers going off to fight for Britain during the war; and *"rousing"* war-time songs the narrator says that were *"reinforced in my brain,"* (p.69). But ironically, it is this colonial education, *"inspired"* by the Empire, which is being used by the narrator to influence her composition for the anthem of *'independence.'*

The reason given is that she *"imitated the strength and vigor of the sentiments it [her colonial songs] offered,"* (p.69). Nonetheless, this is so despite being ignorant of the meaning and content of such songs. This Welsh song, **Men of Harlech**+ is in fact, quite unrelated to the environment because its lyrics date back to England/Wales in 1784. It is a marching song which is something of an unofficial anthem in Wales; its martial air has become identified with Wales's determination to retain its identity.

That being the case, and the fact that a national anthem is to do with inspiring self-determination, independence and claiming one's identity, it's uncanny that Joanne wants to imitate the style of that song for her own version of a national anthem for Grenada.

A further glimpse of the colonial brand of schooling is presented by Mr. Jessup's style of leadership. The imagery of the English Headmaster, as an army-general in khaki uniform, drilling the pupils in the hot sun, and the prominence of the Union Jack flag, as well as a portrait of the Queen, confirm that the Headmaster is doing his duty to England, the *'Mother Country* or *Motherland.'* This also represents the ongoing existence of colonial domination still on the island.

What seems obvious here is that there is continued parroting of information and imitation of styles across succeeding generations: Gran-gran, Aunt Meena and Joanne. Both Gran-gran and Aunt Meena are unsure of the details of the songs they sing, and are unclear about the facts surrounding West Indian soldiers going to fight on behalf of Britain, other than scanty information about people from each parish in the island joining the allies to aid Britain in the war with Germany. Their fading memory is symbolic of the political changes of the day; the outgoing and fading control of *colonialism* and the contrasting incoming *independence in the island*; offering everyone free participation or ownership in a contest to compose the island's own national anthem.

CHAPTER 4 – SUMMARY & ANALYSIS	
CHARACTERS	**RELATIONSHIPS**
Joanne **Gran-gran** **Aunt Meena** **Yvonne, Monica, Lydia**	**Narrator** **Joanne's 70 yr old Grandmother** **Joanne's Aunt** **Aunt Meena's children**
Emma **Daisy** **Mark**	**Children of the village**

Events in this Chapter

1. Gran-gran and Aunt Meena takes turns to supervise the girls since the near-catastrophe with the 'priest.'
2. Aunt Meena, restless and agitated, calls the girls and quizzes them individually over the incident.
3. Aunt Meena replies after each girl's tale, with strong curses in broken French and English; enraged that the 'priest' had gotten away with too much.
4. With the realization of the near-disaster, she single-handedly changes the cultural rules and tradition of calling non-blood-related adults *"auntie"* and *"uncle."*
5. Joanne, who had been imitating her cousins by calling their mother *"Auntie",* now has to call her *"mamie."*
6. It's "*Gloria Saturday*," and the local girls go to the river to wash clothes and catch the excessive amounts of crayfish in the river at this time, based on folk lore.
7. Everyone learns that Emma is next in line to leave Grenada
8. The group of girls discusses their gossips and rumours about migrants having a bad time in England. They try to ponder over the scanty information about how Grenadians are living, being treated and the extreme forms of racism, it rumoured, they endure in England.
9. Emma plans to steal one of Aunt Meena's letters from England to learn more.
10. On their way home from the river, the girls learn about Mark's death and all plans for their *"cook-up"* of the crayfish, pales into insignificance.
11. The incident throws the village into total emotional upheaval.
12. Mark's funeral, the epitome of a local and traditional funeral; is a stark contrast of Irene's funeral in the **Prologue**.

Chapter Summary

This is the period immediately following the 'priest's' departure. Gran-gran and Aunt Meena takes turns to supervise the girls as they are excessively nervous since the near-catastrophe with the 'priest.' We learn about Aunt Meena's character, *a shrewd, business woman, sharp wither tongue in her rebukes, with a school teacher's austerity*

(pp.110) and changeable moods. She is constantly on the alert regarding supervision of Joanne. This is because Joanne has been left in her care by her mother (Meena's sister), who has migrated to England.

Joanne and her cousins, Monica and Yvonne, prepare lunch and everyone, including Blackie the dog, is resting in the heat in the verandah. They greet passers-by but Aunt Meena is restless and agitated. She calls the girls and quizzes them individually over the incident with the priest. The girls are reluctant to talk and she orders them to speak, failing which they will be physically punished. Each girl tells her what the 'priest' did to her. Aunt Meena replies each time with strong pronouncements of broken French curses; enraged that the 'priest' had gotten away with far too much.

With the realization of the near-disaster, Aunt Meena single-handedly changes the cultural rules and tradition of calling people who are not related by blood ***"auntie"*** and ***"uncle."*** Hitherto, this had been a cultural mark of respect and tradition but the 'priest's cunning has taught them that it is a dangerous practice to continue. Aunt Meena explains her reasons for the changes and orders that the new system must take immediate effect. ***"Is not everybody you see is a uncle or ah auntie. There is nothing wrong in saying "mister" or "miss." We have to draw the line and change things up to suit our ways now. Uncle and auntie from now is you blood family," (p.116).*** Joanne, who has been imitating her cousins and calling her mother ***"Auntie,"*** now has to call her mother ***"mamie."*** Aunt Meena's girls have to call her ***"mamie"*** too.

It's a somber time for the family as everyone reflects on the incident with the 'priest' and takes solace in Gran-gran's ***Words of Comfort.*** Aunt Meena conducts a personal, introspective post-mortem on the situation, and feels ashamed at what could have been, intensified by the possibility of her current loss of face and reputation among the villagers.

A few weeks pass and a seasonal event, ***"Gloria Saturday,"*** finds the local girls' going to the river to wash clothes and catch crayfish. Based on folklore, there are usually excesses of crayfish in the river on ***"Gloria Saturday."*** The girls go to St. John's River, where they meet other village children. We learn about the local landscape, the power of nature and its control over the folks, a history of St. John's River, and local lore about the silk cotton tree, which is associated with witchcraft.

Emma is quieter than normal and Joanne is angry, having learnt by chance, that Emma is the next child in line to leave Grenada, with recent news from England. Joanne is shocked and there is tension between the girls. The groups of girls in the river have a general conversation about gossips and rumours of migrants who are having a bad time in England. They try to puzzle through the scanty information about how Grenadians are being treated in England, especially the rumoured extreme forms of racism they're experiencing.

Joanne discovers that, unlike the other girls, she knows very little about what goes on in life, ***"I felt angry that I had been by-passed information but more so that I had never*** *seen the inside of a letter from England,"* (p.128). She plans to steal one of Aunt Meena's letters from England to learn more. She says that in the 6 years that her mother had migrated, the image of her was now more distant, *"she had become like a phantom, like Santa Claus, who had the ability to send presents, nice things,"* (p.129).

The girls learn about Mark's death on their way home from the river and all plans for their *"cook-up"* of the crayfish, pales into insignificance. Mark and his friends were playing on a tractor's wheels, when he slipped and was crushed by the moving machine. The incident throws the village into upheaval, with traditional mourning which seems to create, *"many other little deaths; death of a village, which disturbed its tranquil but jovial routines; the robust women-figures who had been mothering and fathering their children had become temporarily children themselves,"* (p.132).

Analysis

The Chapter focuses on the characteristics and roles of both Gran-gran and Aunt Meena after the 'priest' left the village. However, we are also shown one of the central concerns in the novel - the complex psychology of family life (in Gran-gran and Aunt Meena's household); with emphasis on their coping strategies, as they are left to bring up migrant relatives' children. Their concerns are highlighted with the women's reaction over the incident with the 'priest.' Considering the consequences in the aftermath of the incident, show its impact on different levels:

(1). **Their reputation among villagers** that troubled them the most, ***"it belittled their judgment, reducing the quality of their unblemished Authority among their children. A sense of shame prevailed over their trust in the stranger and the shock that they themselves had been consenting parties,"*** **(p.108).**

(2). **Their individual sense of failure** - did this incident make Aunt Meena feel she had failed in her show of outward 'love' for the children? The narrator says that ***"love was outward defence against threats from outside for our family circle and she did so most vehemently,"*** **(p.110).**

(3). **Their struggles** - This incident brought out the struggles of families in the island, who have to deal with their relative's children and the strain it puts them and those around them. One wonders whether it's because of ***"presiding over surrogate families for absentee parents*** **that made Aunt Meena so uptight, complex and fearful to the children. She had *"no time for emotional exchanges, no "I love you's" and certainly no loving embraces,"* (p.110).**

(4). **Mothering and 'fathering' children** - We know Aunt Meena has an exemplary role of both mother and 'father.' This is because she ***"worked hard on the land which she cultivated for her sister in England"*** **and *"planted and sowed enough food for our need and the surplus was always taken to Grenville market on Saturdays for sale. She was a shrewd business woman,"* (p.110).** However, did her personality changed because of her responsibility to her Sister in England?

(5). **An island-wide problem** - Aunt Meena is never relaxed, with ***"a hardened expression to scold someone with a seriousness that made it difficult to approach her with anything insignificant."*** Although she laughs, "***it was difficult to judge whether they were real or not,*" (p.110).** The narrator tells us that Aunt Meena's demeanour was commonplace among families with similar responsibilities, caring for their relatives children. We learn that it ***"was probably being totally responsible for someone else's child or children was a burden which made it difficult for them to relax, being judged not only the children's parents abroad but the villagers as a whole, who were also "presiding over surrogate families for the absentee parents,"* (p.111).**

It was after the 'priest' incident, that Aunt Meena took matters into her own hands, to announce a break with tradition about how adults in society should be acknowledged by children. She does not consult the elders in the village for discussion or permission, despite the issue being a matter for the folks to also consider. We see her like a Major General, instructing the children as to what aspects of the cultural tradition they should now take on board; fearing that their naivety has exposed them to grave danger and revealed an area of weakness in her coping mechanism.

On another level, there is a sub-text which suggests that despite previous super-power rivalry in the island (French and British rule); and their demise of visible power, a kind of strategic fighting from outsiders continue in society, but via different sources. There is therefore, a subtle suggestion that constant ***vigilance*** is required. On another level, symbolically, the priest could represent subtle imposition by other superpowers in Grenada, and the subsequent action in the island in 1983 by US President Reagan, and the reasons given for such action, allude to such forms of subtlety.

From a cultural point of view, Mark's death, in this Chapter, portrays solidarity among the villagers and presents the cultural role of traditional folks in the island. We learn of the part played by the villagers, people from around the island, which demonstrated togetherness that present the unity among the islanders. We learn that after the announcement on the radio, people, ***"came to commiserate, to support, to cook, share, bring food, take turns in helping others who were paying their respects, and to bawl. It seemed as if the whole of little Grenada had converged in our village, in support of this sad affair,"* (p.132).** The sense of loss is poignantly felt by everyone, especially Mark's family; whose extreme displays of emotions are so uncontrollable, that it instills extreme fear among the children. This funeral is the epitome of a traditional funeral, with its stark contrast of Irene's (the *returning,* migrant, Grenadian) funeral earlier in the **Prologue.**

Another sub-text in this Chapter is the innocent wanderings of the girls as they discuss the plight of the Grenadian migrants in England. The girls' information provide social and migrant history of both Grenada and England. We learn of the racism that migrants faced via public rejection in England, which included a similar fate for ***"Irish"*** and ***"dogs."*** More insights are gained from the information about the basic survival of the folks in England, ***fighting for space on a cooker to cook before the gas they using run out,* (p.124)** and Mr. Mitchell's personal history and of his ***"nigger bashing"*** at the hands of "***Teddy Boys***" who ***"beat him up with some heavy boots, mash up his mouth so he have to wear false teeth,"*** **(p.125*).*** The information we learn about the status of the men and women who left the island **"as *teachers, nurses*"** and found themselves forced **to "*wash shit, clean people house, make up bed, sweep train station, wash dishes,"*** **(p.126)** is reflective of Calvin's story in **Part II** of the novel.

We learn from the girls' information that in England, ***"the people want to fight you because you coloured,"*** **(p.126).** What is clear from the girls' discussion is that the general, widespread expectation and presumption of life in England, does not match the reality of what they were discussing and it was Daisy who asked the all-important question, ***"Why people going there then?"*** **(p.127). The** silence that existed after the unanswered question is the poignancy of their discussion because the narrator says that, ***"No one answered because no one knew the answer to that question,"*** **(p.128).**

CHAPTER 5 - SUMMARY & ANALYSIS

CHARACTERS	RELATIONSHIPS
Joanne	**Narrator**
Gran-gran	**Joanne's 70 yr old Grandmother**
Aunt Meena	**Joanne's Aunt**
Yvonne, Monica, Lydia	**Aunt Meena's children**
Irene	**Aunt Meena's sister, Joanne's mother**
Emma	**Joanne's best friend**
Christopher	**Velma/Manny's son, Miss Cleothilda's nephew**
Miss Cleothilda	**Christopher's Aunt and Velma's sister**
Dr. Japal	**A local medical doctor**
Claudine	**Manny's ex-girlfriend**
Mr. Jessup	**Headmaster – Belair Government School**
Teacher Zoë	**School Teacher**
Rosamond Williams	**School Teacher**
Mr. Franklin	**A neighbour near to the school**

Events in this Chapter

1. Four year old Christopher Smith, who is born in England, is sent to Grenada by his Grenadian parents who are living in England and are facing a family crisis.
2. Most of the information about Christopher is presented as information the narrator overhears in a conversation between Aunt Meena and Miss Cleothilda, Christopher's aunt.
3. Manny, a Jamaican migrant, meets Velma from Grenada and at a Blues party one Saturday night in Ladbroke Grove. Velma later becomes pregnant and when Christopher is born, their Landlord throws them out of their accommodation, saying; ***"he couldn't have them in his house with children,"* (p.142).**
4. Claudine, an ex-girlfriend of Manny in Jamaica, hears about him and believes that he is doing well in England. She writes to him frequently demanding money, and then uses this to buy a ticket for a flight to England, where she turns up unannounced on the couple.
5. Claudine knocks on the couple's door and starts beating up Manny. Velma runs away with little Christopher. As a single mother she is not able to look after the boy, so sends him to her sister in Grenada.
6. Motivated by all this information Joanne steals another letter and learns more about life in England.
7. Emma prepares to leave Grenada for England and Joanne is fearful of losing her best friend.
8. Joanne and Emma recalls being physically punished in front of 500 pupils in their school, as public disgrace, psychological trauma; meant to teach them a lesson in discipline.

Chapter Summary

This Chapter presents the plight of Christopher Smith, a little 4 year old, who is born in England and is sent to Grenada by his Grenadian parents who live in England but are facing a family dilemma. The information about Christopher is information the narrator overhears in a conversation between Aunt Meena and Miss Cleothilda, Christopher's aunt while they are standing in Grenville market.

Miss Cleothilda, being Velma's sister, has first-hand information about Velma and Manny's big bust-up, which was caused by Claudine, an old girlfriend of Manny, who surprisingly turns up on their doorstep in England, unbeknown to the couple.

Before this incident, Manny lives in a room and because of his cultural habit of saying the customary, ***"Good morning"*** and ***"Good evening"*** to people; the landlord's wife misunderstands this as his romantic interest in her. It turns out that the Landlord's wife likes him but Manny is respectful and rejects her advances. Embarrassed by this, she lies to her husband, saying that it is Manny who is making advances at her. As a result, Manny is thrown out of his room. Manny originates from Jamaica, and had met Velma from Grenada, at a Blues party one Saturday night, in Ladbroke Grove. They decide to live together and are in a happy relationship. Velma becomes pregnant and Manny is happy with their situation. Their relation blossoms and all is well, until Velma gives birth to Christopher. Despite being ***"the best rent payers he had ever had,"*** **(p.142)** the Landlord throws them out saying ***"he couldn't have them in his house with children,"*** **(p.142).** Life is on a downturn and they are rejected everywhere they go for similar reasons.

However, their luck changes when one cold, bitter, day Manny meets a fellow school-mate, from Jamaica on Kilburn High Road. During their conversation, he gives Manny information about an available room for rent, which Manny later gets. Being so excited about having met someone from home, Manny's friend writes home to brag about this. The information is shared among the villagers and Claudine, an ex-girlfriend of Manny, learns about this. She somehow gets Manny's address in England and hatches a plan. She writes repeatedly to Manny and extracts money from him, after telling him he is the father of her baby girl. Unclear about the whole scenario, Manny bows to her demands for money, and she extracts not only the cost of a ticket to England but decides to go to England herself.

Meanwhile, Manny, Velma and Christopher lives happily. They take turns to baby-sit Christopher with their working arrangements; one working at night and the other daytime. Their plans to get married and buy a house began with joining a ***Su-su***, to amass lump sums of money. They did not know that trouble was about to threaten their peace because Claudine was hatching her own plans to turn up on Manny's doorstep, unannounced. Claudine arrives in England, Manny opens the door and she notices the trio and their love nest. She physically attacks Manny and beats him up, during which time Velma flees with little Christopher. This information, together with what she had learnt from Daisy and the girls, motivates Joanne to take another of Aunt Meena's letter to learn more about life in England.

After their day in the market Aunt Meena discusses with Gran-gran details of the day's sales. While the women are resting in the Verandah after dinner, Joanne steals another letter and learns more about life in England, which confirms some of what the girls had discussed in St. John's River.

Emma prepares to leave Grenada for England and she is fearful of losing her best friend. The two girls travel the three-mile trek to school, when they reminisce about a Primary school incident which they call "***sapodilla disgrace.***" Joanne and Emma's story recalls being physically punished in front of 500 pupils in their school, as public disgrace, psychological trauma; meant to teach them a lesson in discipline.

The background to the story is that the two exuberant, tomboyish girls had left the school compound one day, to roam around an area where they willfully picked lots of sapodillas, including unripe ones. They were able to dodge a man and his dog; when they thought they had got away with it unnoticed. However, unknown to the girls, they had been seen, and the green sapodillas were collected in a rusted tin and covered with a white, lacy cloth and were brought to their school.

The girls were made to parade through the school assembly with this and were publicly whipped and disgraced in front of the whole school. The girls recall the incident which happened in their primary years. Now years later, the girls are able to laugh at the incident, having adopted the **"*grinning mask*"** to **"*hide the pain they had temporarily resurrected,*" (p.164).**

Analysis

The theme of ***migration*** looms largely in this Chapter, but with children reversing the trend from England to Grenada; from a big economically strong place to a small one. We begin to get the sense that the girls' innocent wanderings and the details of their discussion may have some truth in it, based on the letters Joanne reads.

The theme of ***violence*** is highlighted in this Chapter, with the public humiliation of Joanne and Emma in their school assembly. Violence is presented through the physical beating of the two girls which are intended to inflict pain (physical and emotional), and to instill fear in others. In the novel, physical punishment is endorsed by the State. Therefore, Mr. Jessup, the school Headmaster, administers corporal punishment with a leather belt in front of his 500 student population and there is a sense here that violence is seen a way of dealing with many issues. It adds to the subtle suggestion that the violence in the novel carries over from the physical and psychic violence committed against the race as a whole; that are still perpetuated on a number of levels in society, as we saw earlier in the novel with Sukram; the fighting women on the street; Aunt Meena's physical beating the girls and Calvin's domestic abuse.

CHAPTER 6 – SUMMARY & ANALYSIS

CHARACTERS	RELATIONSHIPS
Joanne **Gran-gran** **Aunt Meena**	**Narrator** **Joanne's 70 yr old Grandmother** **Joanne's Aunt**
Miss Seraphine & Celia	**Villagers**

Events in this Chapter

1. Emma leaves Grenada for England.
2. Joanne, who is lonely as a result, sneaks another of Aunt Meena's letter from England.
3. Joanne discovers more information about life in England and the truth about her past.
4. Randolph's (Joanne's father), sister had made enquiries about Joanne.
5. Irene (Joanne's mother), refused all communication, with the excuse that it would confuse Joanne.
6. Irene, being very resentful, has not forgiven Randolph and his family for their rejection of her and appears still bitter about it; the fact that she has been caring for Joanne herself these past 12 years.
7. Joanne's is disturbed by the upheaval her entry into the world has caused, but is forgiving and feels sorry for the ex-lovers. She plans a mission to rekindle their former love.
8. Aunt Meena returns from Hermitage and relates the story of Celia, (an old friend), to Gran-gran. It's about disputes on land that Celia is looking after for her brother in England and relatives in Grenada, who are willfully defying her Authority.
9. Gran-gran is philosophical about the value of land and makes a profound comment about the land; which she says, is where all must return.
10. Gran-gran projects the different views about land, across the generations.

Chapter Summary

Joanne's best friend, Emma, has left Grenada for England causing Joanne to now have lots of free time on her hands. She takes another of Aunt Meena's letter to find out more about life in England. She hides the letter in her ***Student's Companion*** book to pretend she is studying. In the yard, under a tree Joanne reads the letter and discovers the condition of life for her mother in England: a miscarriage last year; the extreme hard work late at night with excessive tiredness; news of another pregnancy; (despite attempting birth control with a coil) and her other concerns, since it is not Irene's intention to settle in England. Irene also expresses fear for their situation, constrained by the, ***"the little money we getting here is just enough to hide ourselves in a room, with a roof over our head, buy a little food and every now and then send a change for you mamie and the children," (p.167).***

Saraphine, a neighbour, calls on Gran-gran and the two women have a conversation, while Joanne continues to read from the concealed letter; by pretending she is doing school work. As Joanne continues to read, she discovers some personal information she had been desperate to learn about. Irene's letter relates the shame she had brought on her family and saw England as a place where she could make up for her shortcomings. She suspects that her early pregnancy (with Joanne), may have caused her father's death; saying, ***"It's a heavy cross to bear," (p.169)*** shows she is still burdened by this.

Joanne learns about the background to her own entry into the world and the name of her father – **Randolph**. Randolph's sister, Marion, has made enquiries about Joanne. Irene instructs Aunt Meena not to accept any change of heart from Randolph's family, saying ***"leopards don't change their spots," (p.169).*** Irene refers to Randolph as a ***"good-for-nothing," (p.169).*** She relates her past heartbreak, having been left to look after Joanne for 12 years without their support. She appeals to Aunt Meena to refuse communication with Randolph's family, fearing the consequence for Joanne; ***"it will only confuse the poor child brains now, it will just confuse her," (p.169).*** Alternatively, she expects to be married to Calvin, after which time Joanne will be accepted by Calvin as his own child; when she will also bear his name.

Joanne is shocked by the revelation and is emotionally disturbed; ***"A lump came up into my throat and a choking dryness gripped the back of my tongue so that my constant swallowing was attempts to calm the nerves rush I now felt," (p.170).*** The catharsis for Joanne is realizing that her life had caused a catastrophe in the family and the village. ***"My head ached and my pulse raced with the realization that the whole village knew about the disgrace which my life had already caused," (p.170).***

As she recovers, her sadness is for both her mother Irene and Randolph, ***"ex-lovers."*** Joanne's new knowledge of the bitterness and resentment that still exists between her parents, gives her a new mission to rekindle their interest. Joanne says it gives her a sense of belonging, as it, ***"awoke in me a spirit of compassion, forgiveness and an immediate need to delve deeper to find out more," (p.172).***

During this time Gran-gran and Miss Saraphine's conversation is over. Joanne mulls over the information in her mind and watches the activities of mad ants in a nearby nest. Joanne compares her situation to the fate of the ants, being fed and cared for by other ants in their complex world. Joanne feels a little guilt in sneaking out the letters but feels that in time this feeling will pass.

Aunt Meena, who had been out, returns from Hermitage where she met Celia, an old friend. While cooking the evening meal, Aunt Meena relates Celia's predicament to Gran-gran. Relatives are destroying Celia's efforts in a piece of cultivated land that she is looking after for her brother, who is in England. The two women give their opinions about how they would each deal with this predicament. Aunt Meena feels that Celia's brother is taking advantage of her; the fact that she is not paid to look after the land, while his wife's relatives in Grenada ignore Celia's authority, by helping themselves to whatever they want.

We learn about how the land is viewed by West Indians, especially Gran-gran; ***"owning land was a sacred act of possession,"* (p.179)** seen also as ***"lifeblood"*** because it ***"brought food, protected and nurtured; it gave life*** and within it, ***consumed the dusty forms which came from it,"* (p.179).**

Gran-gran states that land should be valued as having more worth than working in an office or migrating abroad and she reasons profoundly, that it is where everyone must return; whether alive or in death. Aunt Meena agrees.

Analysis

We see the continuing exodus of children from Grenada, as part of the stream of migrating nationals pushing outward, to join parents in England. Irene's letter, despite giving information to the contrary, has a tone that suggest that the migrants' level of suffering somehow still perpetuates the view that they are better off in England.

Clearly, England is presented in a kind of double vision. One is based on suppositions, hearsays, gossips and the high expectations of the folks for betterment there. The other is based on information from the economic migrants in England; who document their real life experiences in the form of letters. The two visions are juxtaposed to show the dominance of the prevailing view, that life is still better on the other side; despite the travails of those migrants abroad.

From this we begin to understand Celia's predicament with her sister-in-law's family in Grenada. There is a sense that the ***land*** which Celia's brother has bought while being in England, seem to represent England in Grenada. His family sees it as an extension of England, the produce from the land and all that it represents is theirs for the taking. This perhaps confirms Gran-gran's view about the value of land. Her deep philosophical reasoning on the different and changing views about the land is a poignant expose of folk reasoning between different generations, about the value placed on the landscape as a whole.

Joanne's continuing dilemma has highlighted new twists and turns, in the complex psychology she reveals between her mother Irene and Randolph, her estranged father. This Chapter gives us an insight into Joanne's emotional state and the kind of psychology that keeps driving her to find out about her past. At only 12 years old, her reasoning and instincts to readily forgive shows the strength of her character and need to continue questing for more.

CHAPTER 7 SUMMARY & ANALYSIS	
CHARACTERS	**RELATIONSHIPS**
Joanne **Gran-gran** **Aunt Meena**	**Narrator** **Joanne's 70 yr old Grandmother** **Joanne's Aunt**
Catherine and Sarah	**Joanne's cousins**

Events in this Chapter

1. Joanne has her first menstrual cycle and is unable to deal with it because she was not taught by Aunt Meena and Gran-gran how to.
2. The women find out about Joanne's first period and give her cryptic warnings about not playing with boys.
3. Joanne still wants to help Randolph and Irene reconcile their differences and refuses to believe that there is absolutely no spark of love between.
4. She experiences occasional mood swings
5. She becomes frustrated but thoughts of Gran-gran and her *Words of Comfort* is able to console her.

Chapter Summary

Joanne is in bed reflecting on what she had learnt the day before, from Aunt Meena's letter from England. She is still burdened by the revelation; made worse by the fact that she has no one to discuss her feelings with, certainly not the old folks. She ponders on possible whereabouts of Randolph and Marion (her aunt), and hears her cousins arguing from the next bedroom. Aunt Meena intervenes and scolds the girls.

Joanne is pensive and remains in bed feeling cozy, when she discovers her first menstrual cycle has begun. She is greatly surprised because it had not come in the way that any of her friends had discussed or in the way that she had imagined. She tells us about discussions among the girls, with stories about how they had each seen their first period, as the method through which she learned information about womanhood.

Gran-gran and Aunt Meena had not prepared Joanne for this and we see her panicking and managing the best way she can. She becomes very concerned about how she would approach Gran-gran and Aunt Meena about this, saying, ***"The embarrassment had seemingly swallowed my speech,"*** **(p.185).** Now in the grip of two emotionally charged situations, (revelations about her past and the appearance of her menstrual cycle), she says that things had become ***"too remarkable for me,"*** **(p.185).**

Aunt Meena and Gran-gran finds out about Joanne's period the next day and they are at first very annoyed that she had kept it a secret but soon take matters in hand with a lot of cryptic *do's* and *don'ts* warnings; now that she has *"become a young woman,"* (p.186) Joanne is told she must *"stop talking to boys,"* (p.186) including Justin.

Joanne continues to think about the possibility of helping Randolph and Irene to bridge the gap between them, when she hopes for some sort of reconciliation. She is impatient with the way things have turned out so far, and refuses to accept that there is absolutely no love between the two *ex-lovers*. Joanne has mood swings, *"the pendulum of emotions swung from despair, fear and panic about an old situation,"* (p.188). Joanne misses Emma, who she says would have been able to help her deal with the situation more clearly, and hopes that going to England one day will make things clearer.

Analysis

This Chapter tells us more about the relationship between the trio, Gran-gran, Aunt Meena and Joanne. It reveals a deep-seated fear among the women for the girls in general, as they grow and develop into womanhood. Previously, we learnt that the girls are kept on a tight leash, and concern for them is heightened because of the incident with the 'priest'. However, we discover a deliberate strategy to keep the girls in ignorance; for fear that certain knowledge would bring about inquisitiveness and trouble. It is a strategy which is flawed, as the attempt to hold someone back in certain areas, does not square with wanting that person to have knowledge, experience and success as a *woman of destiny*.

It is not the first time we see the girls trying to solve puzzles about life's issues because they simply do not know the details: (e.g., the **Men of Harlech** song, information about life in England, and how to handle seeing your first menstrual cycle). The children seem to exist on hearsays, gossips, second-hand information, and personal experience, outside of their strict home-church-school routine.

This situation is reflective of the issues (**Chapter 2**), faced by those who are caring and rearing other relatives' children. The result of such forms of upbringing is that things can go really wrong, as we see in Irene and Jessica's case. The fact is, a lack of knowledge fuelled their curiosity and untutored desires, so they became pregnant at an early age; forcing their parents to take some drastic actions as a consequence. On the other hand, it could be the reason behind the passion, (from the lack of information), that drives Joanne to find out more about herself and her past.

CHAPTER 8 - SUMMARY & ANALYSIS

CHARACTERS	RELATIONSHIPS
Joanne Gran-gran Aunt Meena Mr. McDonald	Narrator Joanne's 70 yr old Grandmother Joanne's Aunt A white Estate Owner
Emery Mr. Glover Teacher Date Mr. James	Nephew of the Overseer from an Estate Music Teacher – a white Englishman Probationary Teacher A respected villager
Jeanne & Dessima Calvin, Darris, Darrin	Young village women Joanne's family in England
Cousin Germaine Justin's dad	Villager at Joanne's farewell A local villager
Miss Gisbreth	A white Canadian Missionary

Events in this Chapter

1. Canadian missionaries come to the village during the school holiday and put on activities with a biblical influence.
2. A fierce overseer with his nephew called Emery, stay in the Great House. He likes Joanne but remains only for a short time in the village.
3. Joanne has piano music lessons from Mr. Glover, her school music teacher but Aunt Meena disapproves and Gran-gran agrees. Joanne is strictly monitored and when she is 20 mins late, the lessons are stopped.
4. Joanne criticizes the differences in bringing up girls and boys and recalls Jean and Dessima's fight in public; she sees it as a result of these differences.
5. Joanne prepares for migrating to England and Gran-gran tells her of being rape as a 13 yr old, as a cautionary tale.
6. There is a village farewell for Joanne and Gran-gran gives Joanne last instructions as to how to become the ***Woman of Destiny*** she has projected for her.

Chapter Summary

It is school holidays and missionaries from Canada come to the village hall with holiday activities, which has a biblical focus. The local estate also has a newcomer, a fierce Overseer, whose job is to supervise the estate on behalf of the absentee landlord or owner. The Overseer has a nephew called Emery; a loner who likes Joanne and whose parents had left Grenada for America. As with all the village children with migrant parents, Emery is also waiting to leave Grenada to go to the USA. He is not liked by the village boys, including Justin, who tease him.

On the day of the missionaries' concert, Emery attends and is impressed by Joanne's stage performance. This becomes a talking point between them after the show, just before Emery is whisked away by the driver who had come to collect him. After that time, Emery seems to have disappeared, much to Joanne's disappointment. However, Joanne prepares for a cultural concert at school. At the same time, she is tutored to play the piano by Mr. Glover, a white English music teacher. The piano lessons were given to compensate for not being accepted in the choir.

Aunt Meena disapproves of this but Gran-gran sees it as a great opportunity for Joanne to progress further. It results in a dilemma, as it brings out more anxiety in Aunt Meena, who imposes stricter punctuality rules. When Joanne is 20 minutes late getting home from school one day, Aunt Meena goes looking for her; only to find her strolling down the road with Emery. All music lessons are stopped as a result. Aunt Meena's excuse is that the distance Joanne has to travel is too long, and we hear the narrator's confirmation as to why: ***"perhaps it was every person's nightmare in the country; the burden of looking after a sister or brother who had emigrated across the Atlantic Ocean," (p.197).*** This we are told is ***"more intense if that child was a girl, turned woman, with innocent ramblings, naïve from over-protection and with such ignorance that made her a potential victim," (p.197).***

Joanne is critical about the difference in the way boys are brought up. They have the freedom to roam and ***"conquer"*** girls who are restricted, and seemingly kept ***"in chastity," (p.198).*** She sees this as a fantasy aspect of the culture which is illogical, since girls are expected to have fashionable marriages by these same young men!

Joanne tells the story of a fight between Jean and Dessima over Teacher Date, a young Probationary teacher, unknown to him. Desperate for his attention, the girls brag about any action by the teacher, which they misconstrue as romantic interest. They quarrel about who's receiving the most meaningful attention from the teacher and their arguments escalate into a public fight; with fierce fighting between the women in the street. The fight attracts attention from men in the rum shop and Mr. James stops the brawl.

The narrator is critical about such behaviour and blames it on the way that girls are brought up and the attitude of men towards them. She criticizes men's attitude with an analogy of bees pollinating flowers and ***"littering the villages with little representatives of their conquests everywhere," (p.203).*** Joanne makes comparisons between Irene and Randolph's situation and realizes that it is why Aunt Meena is excessive in her protection to prevent similar occurrences for her; until she is relieved of that burden.

A letter arrives from England and Gran-gran and Aunt Meena learn of Joanne's imminent departure to join Irene, (and members of the family unknown to Joanne) - Calvin and the twins in England. The women talk in ***French* Creole**, as they discuss the news and Joanne notices Gran-gran's ***"pained"*** appearance followed by ***"her nervous eye twitches….more pronounced," (p.205).*** The emotional impact on Gran-gran is that she ***"gritted her teeth and remained sadly silent; biting her lips to control the screaming***

inside her heart,"* (p.205).** The fact that these signs had occurred before, makes Joanne recognize and remember Gran-gran's ***voiceless screams*;* which occurred in ***her childhood after being raped by Mr. McDonald, the white Estate owner,"* (p.206).**

Gran-gran tells Joanne the shocking details of a rape she suffered at the age of 13. Her mother had died leaving their father to bring up 7 children by himself. In relieving Gran-gran's dad of some of the burdens, Mr. McDonald, a white Plantation Estate Owner, had apprenticed Gran-gran at his House as a housekeeper because she could read, as was her great grandmother, (*Wilomena, the Ashanti warrior*) before her.

One day, when no one was around in the house, Mr. McDonald rapes Gran-gran as she is cleaning out his bedroom. He threatens and warns Gran-gran to keep it a secret; telling her that no one would believe her against him, being her boss. Additionally, he threatened that he would tell her father that it was she who teased him sexually. Gran-gran suffers this traumatic experience repeatedly until Mr. McDonald suffers a stroke and dies 18 months later. Gran-gran says it was an answer to prayer after she sought revenge through witchcraft; this she did with the help of Mr. Stan Joseph, the local obeah man. However, though Gran-gran feels that in dying, Mr. McDonald was lucky, since she continues to suffer from the experience manifested as ***"voiceless screams"* (p.205),** made visible by her nervous twitching.

Joanne is surprised that Gran-gran tells her this story and is embarrassed by the details. She tells us that the rape story was used as a caution to Joanne. She feels guilty of finally going to England but secretly looks forward to her departure in April. She ponders over having to deal with a step-father, Calvin and twin sisters, who she has never met and whose surname she would have to adopt. She has concerns about having to call Calvin ***"daddy."***

Bound for the unknown, she recalls that Emma's letters did not paint a rosy picture of England, but had become shorter and lacked excitement. However, the impending, unknown, territory where her uncle, Gran-gran's son had died mysteriously, was still appealing to Joanne. The reality of having to leave Gran-gran and relinquish her reading from the ***Words of Comfort*** left Joanne feeling emotionally distraught because Gran-gran was forced to make preparations for Joanne's departure. Gran-gran learns sections from her ***Words of Comfort*** by heart, and the emotional build up to the eventual parting is heightened.

Joanne's outfit and accessories for travel arrives from England, minus socks which Joanne is pleased about. Gran-gran and Aunt Meena decides to buy these themselves. Joanne carefully selects items to take with her to England and tries to absorb the environment mentally, visibly and via memory, to help her remember after she leaves. Alongside her British passport, Joanne takes school reports, Sunday school work, a bible, her Grenada Independence Medal, French and Spanish text books.

Joanne's last farewell event is comical and solemn at the same time. Justin dad's drunken repertoire provides the comedy, in his speechmaking attempts when he tries to be solemn, oratorical, formal, and intelligent; instead, he rambles, is verbose and is intoxicated, so he makes a hash of the event. Listeners provide the heckling which is equally comical and the event is kept light-hearted.

In contrast, Gran-gran's farewell to Joanne is her own personal **"Words of Comfort"** when she instructs her on the requirements for becoming the ***Woman of Destiny*** that Joanne must become. She relates the qualities needed after giving Joanne some beads which is now being passed down from Gran-gran's mother, an Ashanti warrior. She explains the significance of this and bids Joanne farewell.

Analysis

This Chapter is quite pivotal in the structure of the novel, as it deals with the essence of the novel's title. Here, the characteristics of being ***A Woman of Destiny,*** from Gran-gran's perspective, are clearly elucidated. Gran-gran waits patiently, after everyone, to have the last word. The aim of this strategic approach to ***destiny*** is about character-formation; information given to Joanne, which is meant to become her roadmap, as she will no longer be Gran-gran's trainee in the way that she has been up to this point. In a sense, the student must now put into practice what she has learnt; the final reminders are Gran-gran's guiding principles, to ensure the outcome is successful.

At Joanne's farewell event, Gran-gran gives clear details of the characteristics of what being ***A Woman of Destiny*** entails, and it's what she expects Joanne to embrace in order to succeed. In this Chapter, after all the expressed good wishes from villagers, we see Gran-gran having the last say as the farewell ends; with her own string of advice and emotional farewell to Joanne. Gran-gran goes to great lengths to explain the essence of what being ***A Woman of Destiny*** entails and does so incisively.

Being ***A Woman of Destiny*** has its characteristics in the following **(pp.220/221):**

1. **Tenacity/defiance**; fighting for what you want, ***"Sometimes you have to fight hard to get your way in things."***
2. **Strength** - must be unsurpassable, an example of the Ashanti warrior (Joanne's great-grand mother): ***"My mother was a strong woman. She did never give up."***
3. **Memory** - active remembering: ***"Remember the mortar and the pestle. Be like them."***
4. **Remain unchanging/steadfast or staying power** rather, ***"like the mortar and pestle."***
5. **Refuse to be dominated or suppressed**: ***"Don't let anyone keep you down. If you fall, rise again."***
6. **Being pragmatic:** ***"Never let your heart be troubled."***
7. **Use of the beads/a point of contact**: *"**focusing** on them will help you **dry your tears** and **lift you** up in times of sadness. They will **bring joy** when you have sorrow."*

Although we hear from other adults throughout the novel when they express their wish that Joanne will be ***A Woman of Destiny***, no one has explained what that entails. There is an understanding that whatever success Joanne achieves, it will be a shared one. Therefore, based on various points in the novel as a whole when this is expressed, (including Gran-gran's cautionary tale of being raped at the age of 13), we can assume the ***destiny*** that other villagers refer to, are based on the same sentiments as Gran-gran's explanation and from this standpoint, we can say that Gran-gran's ***voice*** via her explanation, is a ***communal*** one.

In this Chapter, we also learn about the activities of ***'outsiders'*** who have come in the form of Canadian missionaries. Their target audience is also the children of the village and it is yet another attempt to ***'educate'*** the young minds of the island. There appears to be a constant practice, (during school holidays), from such 'outsiders' to bring in their brand of religious dogmas to the island via the children. Miss Gisbreth, the Canadian missionary, is a case in point and it appears to be the village's ***Achilles heels***, because it is also how the villagers were taken-in by the deceptive practices of the 'African priest'.

As another 'outside' influence, the presence of the Great House in the village is symbolic of colonial rule by delegated powers. Great Houses are edifices of colonial dominance in the locality and they were the seats of British Landowners' power in the island. These houses, great in size and the level of business conducted on the island, were the extracting point of the wealth and products from the island's estates for export. Mr. McDonald's sexual abuse of Gran-gran in the local Great House underscores her vulnerability against such dominance; Gran-gran tells us that she sought the help of witchcraft from a local *obeah man* to deal with her powerless situation. Towards the end of colonial rule, many of these houses were occupied by local Overseers with delegated powers to run the Estates, with an iron fist, on behalf of their absentee Landlords.

This is the last Chapter of **Part I** of the novel, and it portrays Joanne as someone who has changed from the passive little girl, to someone whose characteristics for **"*destiny*"** is already being formed. In this Chapter, Joanne is maturing; she is becoming more vocal and is now more aware of her surroundings. She criticizes the differences in the up-bringing between girls and boys, and exposes the folly of unrestrained freedom for boys to roam and the contrast of keeping girls **"*in chastity,*" (p.198).**

Then in a profound manner, she questions who the expected partner of the 'chaste' girls will be, when as potential husbands, they are being trained to be ***saga boys.*** Joanne links this dilemma with Jean and Dessima's story to show the result of such folly; especially since the women feel that the teacher is comparatively rare and a potentially good 'catch'. This tone and maturity of reasoning signals Joanne's developing sensibilities as she leaves the folks and Grenada's landscape behind. After all, as master narrator, she is also a commentator on the behaviour of others in the novel and also on the wider situation in Grenada and England.

PART II

CHAPTER 9 - SUMMARY & ANALYSIS	
CHARACTERS	**RELATIONSHIPS**
Joanne **Irene** **Calvin** **Darris & Darrin**	**Narrator in England** **Joanne's mother** **Joanne's stepfather** **Joanne's twin sisters**

Events in this Chapter

1. Joanne finally leaves Grenada, travelling via Barbados to England.
2. She reaches England and feels terrorized by the coldness of the weather and people at Heathrow Airport.
3. At the airport, she meets her mother who has an ***unfamiliar voice* (p.225)**, after a gap of 9 years.
4. Joanne is taken to her new home where she meets her stepfather, Calvin and twin sisters, Darris and Darrin; who she shares a bedroom with.
5. She settles into a mundane routine and is lonely; feels penned in because her mum has a night job, which necessitates sleeping during the day, leaving Joanne to look after the twins, who go to school each day. Calvin is unemployed.
6. Joanne is not allocated a school and in the first month of not going anywhere she is excessively bored.
7. In desperation to get out of the house, Joanne agrees to pick up the twins from school.
8. She quickly discovers England is not what she had imagined and loses her way while trying to reach the twins' school.
9. This experience makes Joanne appreciate the differences in Grenada and regrets leaving the island.

Summary

Joanne leaves Grenada, travelling to Barbados on a LIAT plane, where she changes on to a BOAC flight to England. She arrives in Heathrow Airport to temperatures that are 15°C, in the care of Flight Attendants. The first thing that's noticeable in the new environment is the ***"cold that made her shiver uncontrollable at the strange chill which prevailed everywhere,"* (p.223).** Her biggest moment in the long-awaited visit to England was on a ***"dull grey day with biting fierce wind, were England's weather greeting at Heathrow,"* (p.225).**

Immediately, she makes comparisons between the two environments and tells us that the cold weather makes her ***whole body shake, teeth clatter and stomach queasy,* (p.224).**

Joanne tells us that she is surrounded by ***angry-looking and unfriendly faces and felt threatened by unfamiliar bodies who don't say Morning or Howdy-dos. "The air felt cold and I was alone," (p.224).*** Compared with the **"*hustle-bustle*"** in Barbados and Grenada, everything is ***"relatively quiet,"*** in the whole environment, which ***"increased the terror*" (p.224)** she was feeling. While waiting to be picked up by her mother, she is extremely anxious and is fearful that perhaps no one will come to collect her. Later, an Air Hostess introduces Joanne to Irene, her mother, who she feels awkward with. Joanne greets her but ***"releases her hold at once"*** as the ***unfamiliarity of her [Irene] voice* made her *speechless," (*p.225).**

They get into a black cab which Joanne compares to a La Croix funeral hearse in Grenada and on the way to her new home, it rains. Joanne notices various differences in her immediate surrounding – the houses, road, driver, the car environment, and vehicles that they pass; and she compares the stark contrast of a similar journey to Pearl's Airport as she was leaving Grenada, less than 24 hours ago.

She describes the journey from her home on the last day in Grenada to Pearls Airport. There is much noise and the crowds of people leaving Grenada as a ***"stampede of passengers and families pressed and hurried inside." (p.228).*** Her departure is hastened, ***"ushered by quick movements and a seriousness of attitude," (p.229).*** The image of her final parting from Aunt Meena and Gran-gran is heart-wrenching and she is ***"swooped up from Grenada's soil... reminiscent of a finished cricket match, a sort of anti-climax, until the next play-off," (p.231).***

Joanne arrives at her new home with her mum, who works at night. She is introduced to Calvin, her stepfather who would now be her ***"daddy"*** and the twins, Darris and Darrin, who give her a pair of slippers. She is unsure whether to be formal or informal with them.

After breakfast, she asks where Brixton is, as it is the area where Emma lives. As she settles into her new home of routines, she feels ***"penned in"*** or ***"caged like a bird" (p.235)*** within the confines of their house; since she is not allocated a school during the first month. The time spent was ***"quiet solemn days" (p.236),*** so she sets off to work on her self-improvement. There is a tinge of regret as she is lonely, bored, feels homesick for Aunt Meena, Gran-gran and the folks. Hers was a ***"solitary world" (p.237)*** so she attempts to venture out to collect the twins from school one day.

She experiences difficulties when, despite thinking she could find her way by marking the areas mentally, she realizes that the ***"sameness"*** everywhere confuses her. She gets lost and becomes anxious about the twins who would be waiting for her at their school to be collected. She becomes angry, frustrated, and regrets thinking that her life was better outside of Grenada. She longs to be in Grenada and now realizes that the variety of everything in Grenada is ***"the creator's unique gift to us, a blessing," (p.238).***

Once it was obvious that the twins were left behind at school, Calvin was called to collect them and lucky for Joanne they were safe at home, when he eventually made her way back home.

Analysis

In this short introductory Chapter to **Part II**, Joanne is approximately 14 years old and for her, the difference in landscapes between Grenada and England is painfully obvious. This Chapter depicts a scene of ***broken rhythm*** in Joanne's storytelling. The reader has just come from the vibrancy and liveliness of the folks, who provide a strong sense of the ***group narration/song*** or Joanne's ***backing band*** in the hot, Grenadian landscape, to a slight pause or change of direction or tone. The language used to describe the new landscape is reflective of that change. Strong adjectives are used when Joanne summarises England: ***cold, anxiety, isolation, strangeness, chill, fearful, traumatized, threatened, invaded, dull, biting, helplessness, terror, abandoned, fierce and unfriendly;*** sums up Joanne's first impression. Even the cab which takes her and Irene home is compared to a funeral hearse!

We get the immediate sense of a ***solo composition,*** which starts off almost as a ***lament,*** already with a tone of regret. Because the new environment is so quiet, Joanne notices there are no greetings of **"*Morning or howdy-dos*" (p.224)** and sounds that would normally be lost, are almost screaming at us. She tells us of her ***pulse racing*** and ***heartbeats pounding,* (p.224)** when the word **"*home*"** was uttered, ***the teeth chattering, and body shaking; heart skipping beats,* (p.224)** feeling the ***heat around her legs*** in the cab, with ***no music;*** even the noticeable ***moving red numbers* (p.226)** on the cab's electronic fares meter.

The harshness of the English weather, which pervades the opening scene in England at Heathrow Airport, may be symbolic of the impending life of difficulties for Joanne the ***soloist***, later in the novel. In this Chapter it is so quiet, that all our senses are engaged at once; when Joanne wakes up to the **sound** of the pilot's in-flight message, **feeling** a stiff and painful neck, her nose **felt** cauterized, she **eyed** other passengers, her head and belly **felt** as if they had exchanged places. She **smells** bacon when greeting her mother for the first time, and later they **ate** breakfast after her arrival at her new home.

It's almost as if the ***music in Joanne's composition has paused*** while she **listens** and prepares for a ***different rhythm and beat***. Her mind skips back to the ***fast rhythm*** of the *Calypso* that was played on her way to the airport in Grenada less than 24hrs ago, and she ***sings/narrates the lyrics*** of two verses. It is almost as Joanne wants to hold on to the voice of the community via the cautionary tone of the Calypsonian **(*the people's mouthpiece*)**; who is advocating the importance of **"*remembering.*"** ***"I say remember who used to hug and kiss, you, don't forget your mother and father!"* (p.227).** The words of the *song* are emphatic, it reasons, it's imperative and reflects on one of the characteristics of Gran-gran's definition of **"*destiny.*"**

The lengths of the Chapters in **Parts I** and **II** are significant too. The novel is framed by two parts: **Part I** is reflective of many voices from a whole village, headed by Gran-gran and Aunt Meena taking charge of Joanne's youth. The Chapters in these early sections of the novel are therefore longer. In contrast, **Part II** portrays Joanne's dominant voice, where she will demonstrate the effectiveness of what she has learnt in **Part I** as she narrates her story.

Therefore, in the **Prologue** and **Epilogue**, she provides a summary of the journey towards her ***destiny*** up to these points and leaves us to conclude whether she has or is still on track to becoming the ***"woman of destiny"*** that has been declared over her life. The opening details of **Part II** could therefore be seen as the symbol of a new beginning for Joanne; whose ***narration/song*** will grow and develop, just as Joanne will do, in the new environment. What happens from here is a turning point, as we are now introduced to issues related to England, as opposed to Grenada.

Immediately Joanne arrives in England, we see her engaged in a different type of domestic chore, especially as her mother ***"was too tired to talk,"*** **(p.235).** She has been catapulted from an environment where she was one among many children being cared for, into one where she now takes a leading role in the home and helps to care for her siblings.

Joanne describes her initial feelings at home as being, ***"penned in by wooden fencing and a padlocked back door;*** **(p.235)** restricted by ***"the confines"*** of their bedroom, **or** ***"revolving between the upstairs/downstairs"*** space of the house; ***"being caged like a bird,"*** **(p.236);** all which give the sense of a person wanting to escape. The language here signifies an imagery of **entrapment** and is reinforced by the additional role she plays in Calvin and Irene's relationship; passing information from one to the other because there is ***"very little congeniality"*** **(p.236)** between them.

Therefore, it is possible to conclude that when Joanne volunteers to collect the twins from school, it could be seen as an attempted **escape**. She becomes a desperate person, whose ***"head ached from the regrettable loneliness and sadness of this little prison world,"*** **(p.237).** Luckily, she is able to overcome such difficulties with "***Gran-gran's memorable words, holding the beads,"*** **(p.237)** which helps her to ***"regain her composure,"*** **(p.237).** Thus, the groundwork for ensuring her development of character into the "***Woman of Destiny,"*** having begun in this new environment; Joanne will continue to narrate her experiences.

CHAPTER 10 - SUMMARY & ANALYSIS

CHARACTERS	RELATIONSHIPS
Joanne	**Narrator in England**
Irene	**Joanne's mother**
Calvin	**Joanne's stepfather**
Aunty Mary	**Irene's sister and Joanne's aunt**
Peter	**Joanne's cousin, Aunty Mary's son**

Events in this Chapter

1. Joanne takes an opportunity to scrub her mum's back during a bath time, to learn about her mum's problems.
2. She is still not at school and Aunty Mary warns her about accepting offers of a place in an ESN school, having been in England longer than her sister.
3. Joanne reminisces about life in Grenada and learns to cope with her isolation.
4. Calvin has conflicts at work; he refuses to do jobs he considers to be menial.
5. Irene is concerned and during a conversation with Aunty Mary, she learns of strategies she could take to avert financial disasters with Calvin's unemployment.
6. Irene joins a ***Su-su*** and begins to save weekly sums of money – Calvin finds out and disapproves.
7. Problems develop; he slaps Irene after a verbal battle between them when Calvin says that her ideas of buying a house in England are ***"crazy."***
8. Their problems are not isolated, as it's widespread among Caribbean people in England.
9. Peter, Joanne's cousin, concludes that marrying a white partner is a solution to these problems.

Summary

Joanne is called to scrub her mum's back and she takes the opportunity to learn anything from her mum; as she did with Gran-gran in Grenada. However, the content of mum's stories was woeful and it was always about work. Joanne listens to problems about her mum's workplace and continues to narrate the stark contrasts and changes she finds in England - at home and in church; compared to Grenada.

Her overriding concern is not having a school to go to and her mother tells her that they must be cautious of being sent to an ESN[2] school. It would seem such schools are being made out to be satisfactory, but Aunty Mary cautions against accepting an offer to go there. Aunty Mary has been in England longer than Irene and her opinions are mostly taken on board; especially as her son Peter had passed five GCEs[3]. We learn that GCE exams are higher than CSEs[4] and Irene is expecting from Joanne results which are similar to Peter's.

Joanne reminisces about her life in Grenada and devises mood-games to help her fill the vacuum she feels, as well as sleeplessness. She tells us that it is Gran-gran's ***Words of Wisdom*** that invades her mind and helps her to plan her future strategies. She is beginning to understand what her grandmother has been telling her, so she declares those positive sentiments defiantly, **"*I will be best of something,*" (p.243).** Joanne's internal and external worlds are at odds – so she uses the internal strength based on her upbringing to deal with her present difficulties.

Then she overhears a disagreement between Calvin and Irene about money. Calvin is at risk of losing his job due to constant conflicts at work with is superiors. He aspires to be a solicitor but Irene's concern is about how he would support the family. We learn that **"*jobs are hard to come by for coloureds,*" (p.243)** and migrants feared this the most – for the employed and the unemployed.

The predicament of migrants is stated clearly in this Chapter and we learn that their lives are dominated by concerns about work, **"*Work dominated every conversation, in every family and when the subject of racism was included, it took second place,*" (p.243/4).** Landlords were callous and do not like Coloured aspirants, who don't want to settle to do any job. However, the discussions function as a kind of bridge-builder and help to maintain relationships among friends and migrant islanders.

Irene and Aunt Mary have a discussion, while knitting garments, about Byron who had lost his job. Byron it seems, has a similar problem to Calvin; his position in Grenada was higher than the menial job he is expected to do in England. ***"He can't stand being a nobody in England washing dishes when he was a big "hefe in Grenada,"* (p.246).** Calvin it seems has decided to "***take two days off work, as sickness, to punish his supervisor,*" (p.247).** Aunty Mary cautions Irene and advises her to take precaution and prepare for eventualities by joining a ***Su-su*** that a friend called Matthew is conducting. The women reason that if Irene could save two shillings periodically into a fund, it could ensure financial stability for the family.

Additionally, Aunty Mary tells Irene about a job at the airport that she heard about that could help her sister if she was able to reorganize her working life to a day job, in order to accommodate the children's school times. All these plans are made without referral to Calvin, it would seem, and he learns about the ***Su-su*** Savings Plan six weeks later. He is furious about the money that is saved behind his back and does not approve of Irene's plan that they buy their own house in England. He sees it as, ***"a foolish ambition, impossible by Coloured standard,"* (p.349).**

Irene does not agree with him and there are sharp words between the two, which develop into physical blows. Calvin slaps Irene, followed by "***scuffling and a noisy quarrel through a tearful voice,*" (p.350).** Irene believes that it's possible to be successful in England and hers is a different experience from Calvin. He reiterates that he is ***"the man in the house"* (p.351)** and storms out of the house angrily.

Joanne's cousin, Peter, is born in England of Grenadian parents, and having assessed the situation among families, concludes that he is better off with a white partner.

Analysis

In this Chapter, the writer allows us to focus on Joanne's reaction to situations around her and shows us her coping strategies. She is a young girl who has to grow up very quickly, placed in an 'adult' environment. She is forced to take on an adult role as she becomes the communicator between Calvin; her step-dad and mother. She continues to overhear information and through this narrative style, we learn about the kind of life led by the Grenadian/Caribbean migrants in England.

Aunty Mary's character portrayal is interesting, as she is almost like a Gran-gran figure, who quietly instructs, guides and uses her knowledge, (having been in England longer then the others), to reason with her sister. She represents **a *master Calypsonian*** in her own right, and ***her voice is one of caution, verbal defence and giving good sense***. She warns Irene about the dangers of accepting an offer of placement for Joanne if it is in an **ESN** school. **ESN** means **"*educationally sub-normal*"** and her warning demonstrates that Aunty Mary is conversant with current issues affecting migrants and is able to steer Irene and Joanne way from serious consequences of wrong actions. She also represents a kind of keeper or transmitter of cultural traditions in the Diaspora, when we see her advising Irene about joining the ***Su-su*** and about the need for economic stability. She doesn't only advise but is also proactive in accompanying her sister to see Matthew, the person organising the ***Su-su*** Savings Plan.

The women try to resolve their issues in silence; which is symptomatic of the way that life is led in England by migrants. **"*Silence and niceties dominated*" (p.243)** Calvin and Irene's relationship. It is also what Joanne recalls when she had first arrived at Heathrow airport; it is what she experiences at home and notices between her mother and aunt. The women ponder their difficulties in quietness while knitting and Joanne tells us **"*as children we learned by listening,*" (p.244).**

However, the content of what they listen to seems to be dominated by problems to do with employment. In other words, their problems are about surviving in their environment. The migrants' stories bring a tone of ***lament or ballad,*** into the narrative, as they seem to ***sing their blues.*** Knitting, Joanne tells us, has a multi-function for both her Aunt and mother; firstly it was an ***art***, which ***consumed*** their free time but also an advantage in ***their economies of scales***. Therefore, they found ways of prioritizing their many responsibilities of not only surviving for themselves and their children but also financially supporting children and families back at home in Grenada.

We get the impression that life is about struggles for survival and everyone gets caught up in the pervasive discussions about work. Joanne tells us that thematically, **"*work reigned supreme*;" (p.244)** meaning, there is very little time for focusing on anything else.

This helps us to understand Joanne's desperation which becomes acute, as she has to constantly ask when she will go to school, rather than the information being volunteered to her. Locked in such an environment, Joanne summons the next best thing to her rescue - Gran-gran's ***Words of Comfort*** and activates her memory; that of "***remembering***." It is noteworthy that one of the characteristics of being that ***Woman of Destiny*** she is empowered to be requires the act of ***"remembering."*** This gives a sense that Joanne already carries the sum total of what it takes to be that ***Woman of Destiny*** within her and therefore application of the rules and guidelines is what will test her mettle and help her to succeed in her cause.

Calvin thinks that his life is harder for him in Britain; being both a male and Black compared with being a Black female. He suggests that there is a difference in negative treatment between Black males and females. However, Irene wants economic and family stability; Calvin wants personal elevation, which he translates as ***"doing better."*** He wants to be a solicitor, and repeats that it's difficult ***"being a Black man"*** **(p.250)** in England.

The women, it seems, are more compromising with their situations in England and are impatient with their men's attitude and defiance. Joanne tells us how the women ***"find answers to their problems"*** **(p.249)** bogged down by greater dissenting forces outside of their domestic situations. Families are in constant battles about the multitude of treatment they get: Landlords' racism; their prejudice about having children in their homes; fears about becoming unemployed and the perpetual nightmare feelings that employment could end abruptly or for those who are unemployed, the reality that ***"jobs were hard to come by for coloured,"*** **(p.243).**

Therefore, we can conclude that the migrants' problems are much more than mere domestic issues because they originate from a wider frame of reference – society in general. Joanne notices and tells us that her family seemed, ***"as if they were carrying the problems of England on their shoulders,"*** **(p.250).** Additionally, these problems were widespread, and not only among Grenadians because ***"the social ills of Caribbean life in Britain had long taken its toll on most black families,"*** **(p.251).** We can see Peter's thoughts and stated choice of partners as a fall-out from such difficulties; though as suggested, one which could present other societal difficulties for Peter.

CHAPTER 11 – SUMMARY & ANALYSIS

CHARACTERS	RELATIONSHIPS
Joanne	**Narrator in England**
Irene	**Joanne's mother, A Vending Operator**
Mrs Alexander	**Irene's Manageress at work**
Shirley, Eileen, Chris	**General Assistants at work**
Rose	**Waitress to the Directors at work**
Ricky	**Chef**

Events in this Chapter

1. Irene has changed her job and is taken on as a Vending Operator in a firm. She is quickly promoted.
2. Her female boss is about to retire and the other workers are jealous and fearful that Irene will be the Manageress' replacement.
3. Ricky, the Chef, becomes the Manager (although he is unsuitable for the post); just to please the General Assistants, who are racist towards Irene. Racism grows stronger among the workers when Nadeen, another foreigner, joins the team.
4. Rose, the self-elected leader among them, champions the racist jibes and growing resentment against Irene, who is growing in popularity.
5. Irene suffers especially when she is bypassed for promotion and Ricky becomes Manager, in name only. Irene is expected to prop up Ricky, who is unable to do the administrative paper work.
6. Ricky's new Authority is disregarded and Rose spearheads the corruption and laxity with the others, including her husband; who turns up, gets free food and hangs around as he pleases. Additionally, she helps to force Nadeen out of her job, so that her unemployed friend could get the job instead.
7. While things fall apart in the workplace, Ricky's marriage problems escalate at home and he seeks Irene's advice. Rose is racially abusive to him, branding him a ***"nigger lover,"* (p.263).**
8. Situations come to a head when Rose breaks down while drunk at work and sobs, during which she says that she just, ***"wants is to be Irene's friend,"* (p.263).** This shocks her colleagues.
9. Irene's leadership comes to the fore when she advises them to use the weekend to consider what has happened.

Summary

Irene is a Vending Operator who has been promoted to being a Cashier within two months of starting her new job. Her boss is Mrs. Alexander, the Manageress of a number of workers who are resentful of Irene's rising promotion and amiable relationship with the Manageress. Despite the work being demanding and ***"nerve-taxing,"* (p.254)** Irene's co-workers are jealous of her position and are fearful that she might be promoted to Manageress, with Mrs. Alexander's imminent retirement.

Shirley gossips in the kitchen with the General Assistants (G.A.s) about Irene, who catches them red-handed. Mrs. Alexander publicly shows confidence in Irene and the girls' resentment grows. Rose is nervous that they will be by-passed in favour of Irene and she has an outburst which reveals that she has issues not only at work but at home. The General Assistants feel Irene should be doing dishwashing and mopping, not the clerical work she is seen doing, and are incensed by the situation. Their feelings grow worse when Nadeen, another foreigner, joins the company. Rose elects to taunt Irene and tries to incite racist feelings among the other workers against Irene.

Irene suffers especially when the girls almost succeed in conspiring against her. However, the GAs are relieved when staff changes make Ricky the new boss. Irene becomes Cashier Control Clerk, and Assistant to Ricky. The girls are jubilant with the changes and no longer see Irene as a threat since she is not their boss. However, Irene overhears a conversation between Mrs. Alexander and Ricky and learns that although she was more suited for the job, Mrs. Alexander chose not give Irene the position because the General Assistants would not approve of the promotion.

Instead, Ricky is given the job and Irene is selected to be his 'backbone' of support because he cannot do the required paperwork to administrate, whereas Irene can. With Ricky becoming boss, the General Assistants disregard his Authority. The mutinous Rose incites Shirley and Chris to do her bidding; discipline breaks down, and Ricky who has added problem with his marriage, is unable to keep a tight rein on the GAs. Rose causes Nadeen to lose her job so that her unemployed teacher friend can get it. Recklessness and corruption is the order of the day and Rose dominates the scene at work: meaning, her husband is able to turn up at her workplace when he wants; he gets free food and hangs around their department, unnoticed by senior Company staff.

Irene is Ricky's **"*tower of strength*" (p.262)** as he is unable to cope well with his worsening marriage situation and his job. Rose is unhappy that the two get on well, so she racially abuses Irene. Rose develops an excessive drinking habit, Ricky's marriage problems worsen and the General Assistants steal, continuously, from the Company.

One day, Rose breaks down while drunk at work and verbally attacks Ricky, saying that he is a **"*nigger-lover*" (p.263).** She is racially abusive and while sobbing, shocks the rest of the staff when she tells Irene, ***"I only want to be your friend,"* (p.263).** The GA's are puzzled and ashamed, as they are now clearer about the whole situation. Irene pities them and tells them to use the approaching weekend to reflect on what has happened so far.

The ***theme of racial prejudice*** in this Chapter is presented as a universal theme of people's intolerance of others. In the novel, there are two instances of racial prejudice; (the encounter of the group of Grenadian children with the Caravan Hiring Company and Irene and the General Assistants in her work-place). This is used to show an example of people's complex inhumanity to others. Located in **Part II** of the novel; where there is interaction between English and ***"foreigners,"*** it shows these instances of prejudice as the real antagonist of those who are enlightened. Neither of these instances dominate the novel, but are interwoven structurally, to complement characterization, especially Calvin, Irene, Peter, perhaps Darris and Byron in **Part II** of the novel.

Analysis

In the previous Chapter, we learnt about the struggles and difficulties faced by the migrants in England. Up to this point, we only hear snippets of information about individuals; what they think and what others think about their dilemmas. For example, from discussions among the children in Grenada, Aunt Meena's letters from England, from Miss Cleothilda and Aunt Meena's gossip in La Bay, tête-à-têtes among Aunty Mary and Irene. However, in this Chapter, the Author allows us to experience with Irene, an example of the wide-spread fears and worries that lead to the ***"social ills"*** of migrants' life in Britain.

When we read about Irene's dilemma in the work-place, we get a deeper insight into her character and begin to understand how she extends her leadership qualities in her home life. Calvin, her ex-husband says in **Chapter 10**, that black women are treated differently from black men. We see Irene in a position of leadership at work, where she demonstrates an unswerving ability to achieve her ambition by being steadfast and uncompromising in her determination to succeed.

Irene is able to withstand her work colleagues' racism and conspiracies; despite feeling ***"overwrought by the hard, nerve-taxing job; work which demanded tact and a pleasing personality,"* (p.254).** Therefore, when she told Calvin to, ***"Go to hell with your pride!"* (p.250),** it was perhaps suggestive of a different way that migrants should deal with their problems in England. She is an over-comer because ***"pride"*** does not take priority over her immediate needs. Her insistence that, ***"We have to make it right here,"* (p.250)** displays tenacity and shows her driving passion to succeed at all cost.

It is noteworthy that she has come a long way in achieving her ambition to become a house-owner in England. She is now a single mother, ***"a divorcee, house-owner with total responsibility for her family,"* (p.254)** who took her sister's advice in **Chapter 10** that, ***"You have to stoop to conquer sometimes,"* (p.245).** Calvin on the other hand, was not prepared to do this. Although we do not get an opportunity to see Calvin in his working environment, we learn that he was not willing to 'climb down, in other to eventually climb up,' based on Aunty Mary's proverbial wisdom of ***"stooping to conquer,"* (p.245).**

One of the underlying issues in this and the previous Chapter, is to do with coping strategies among migrants in England. Both Calvin and Byron were impatient with their individual situations; influenced by the fact that they both held higher positions in Grenada before going to England, and are now unwilling to take menial jobs to survive. However, it appears their pride and need as individuals, took priority over their immediate and extended family needs. Seemingly, they overlooked the reality that

England does not have ***"a money-tree"*** **(p.246)** or, the understanding that despite what you personally want, the choice is ***"you work or starve,"*** **(p.246).**

Calvin's way of coping with his situation at work is to confront or ***"punish them,"*** **(p.247)** by taking days off-work, pretending to be sick. In other words, he continues to be in conflict with his "superiors" at work, without a fall-back position or workable alternative. Logically, it's a battle Calvin cannot win because in addition to there being a ***"shortage of jobs for coloureds"*** **(p.243),** he also needs to maintain whatever job he has and make advance plans for his exit; (prioritizing his family's financial needs). He does not have another job to go to so it would mean a break in employment; jeopardizing his ability to look after his family adequately. Irene's outburst to Calvin's pessimism in the previous Chapter when they argued was, ***"at least mine [plan] is practical,"*** **(p.250).** Therefore, we get the sense that she is a planner and a doer, rather than someone who just articulates a desire.

In reality, Irene was by-passed for the promotion of Manageress at work and we are told she is a most suitable candidate, who apparently was being trained for the position. Irene ensures she is tolerant of all situations, despite their obvious psychological complexities. However, in spite of her suitability for the promotion, she is blatantly overlooked; and Ricky, who is less qualified and unable to do the job, is given the promotion. Conversely, Irene is used as a cover-up for Ricky's inability to administrate, just to please the rest of the workers and to stave off a racist rebellion against Irene as Manager.

As a single parent, Irene maintains her own home and takes care of her family and still undertakes her duties at work. Despite these layers of responsibilities, when things fall apart at work, Irene is the only one who can 'hold the fort,' supervise, guide and still empower the workers.

If we return to Gran-gran's characteristics as outlined for Joanne, in becoming a ***Woman of Destiny,*** it is possible to see some of these qualities in Irene. For example, Irene has displayed five out of Gran-gran's seven qualities needed, as follows **(pp.220/221):**

- **Tenacity/defiance;** fighting for what you want, ***"Sometimes you have to fight hard to get your way in things."***
- **Strength** - must be unsurpassable, an example of Willomena, the Ashanti warrior (Irene's grand mother): ***"My mother was a strong woman. She did never give up."***
- **Remain unchanging/steadfast or staying power** rather, ***"like the mortar and pestle."***
- **Refuse to be dominated or suppressed**: ***"Don't let anyone keep you down. If you fall, rise again."***
- **Being pragmatic:** ***"Never let your heart be troubled."***

Irene is a ***"tower of strength"*** **(p.262)** to Ricky her boss and appears to be unperturbed by her work colleagues' racism and intense dislike of her. She adheres to good working principles and as a result, it is those qualities that appear to be both attractive and repellent to Rose. Despite her outward appearance of hatred and racism, Rose's admiration for Irene is borne out in her surprising statement, ***"I only want to be your friend!"*****(p.263).** Irene therefore emerges as someone who, like her daughter Joanne, could also be a ***Woman of Destiny***.

Racial prejudice in this Chapter is presented as a universal theme of people's intolerance of others. This is used to show an example of people's complex inhumanity to others. Despite being a Chapter about Irene's experiences at work, it does not dominate the novel, but is interwoven structurally to complement Irene and Calvin's characters and to give an insight into the backdrop of their domestic situation.

CHAPTER 12 - SUMMARY & ANALYSIS

CHARACTERS	RELATIONSHIPS
Joanne	**Narrator in England**
Irene	**Joanne's mother**
Aunty Mary	**Joanne's aunt**
Miss Hubbard	**The Head teacher**
Jessica	**A Grenadian student who's sent to a ESN school**

Events in this Chapter

1. Joanne finally gets a school placement, and finds the work much easier than her previous education level in Grenada. As a result, she is forced to give up French and take up Shorthand, which is a new subject.
2. She is passionate about learning in this local school, led by Miss Hubbard, a strict disciplinarian, whose strictness results in a Jessica, a Grenadian girl going to an **ESN** school.
3. The English cookery menu presents a problem; especially the need to create a menu for a ***High Tea*** **(p.267)**, not only for Joanne and her immediate family but Aunt Mary also, who don't know what a ***High Tea*** is.
4. Joanne attempts to make contact with Emma, but does not succeed.
5. Joanne settles down to her ***English " home"*** **(p.269)** and comes to realise that the term **"*home*"** has taken on a new meaning.
6. As Joanne grows, her circle of friends widens and one summer a small group of them, (migrant children), decide to go to the West Country on holiday.
7. She narrates how, having made friends, they sought to enjoy their life in England; by exploring and **"*venturing into other parts of the country,*" (p.269).**
8. They encounter both overt and subtle forms of racism trying to hire a caravan which marred their holiday.
9. The group has a discussion about various contrasting points of views, expressed by each member, based on life experiences in England.

Summary

After months of waiting, Joanne eventually gets a school placement at a local girls' school. She finds the standard of education lower than her previous level in Grenada. So instead of waiting in the class for her classmates to catch up to her level of French attainment, she gives it up to choose an alternative subject. Joanne's choice is Shorthand and her thirst for knowledge which increased during the months of waiting to start school, created an obsession for learning.

She is tenacious in her application to her studies and this delights her teachers, especially Miss Edwards, her Pitman Shorthand teacher. She tells us that, ***"every teacher admired my passion to soar in my educational endeavours and this was the talk in the staff room,"* (p.267).** However, she becomes unstuck with Cookery homework that required her to create a menu for a ***"High Tea."*** Neither, Joanne, her mother nor Aunty Mary knows what a **High Tea** was. Joanne feels ***"defeated"*** and embarrassed at everyone's lack of knowledge and her own sense of disappointment.

The school has a strict environment, led by Miss Hubbard, a disciplinarian and old-fashioned Headmistress. She warns against those who break the rules on social etiquette, especially encouraging boys to come to the school gates and also warns against girls' fighting on school premises. There is a known culprit, Jessica, a Grenadian girl, who was later sent to an **Educationally Sub-Normal** (**ESN**) school; the kind that Aunty Mary had warned Irene against.

Joanne quips about **ESN** schools, and questions why the British government's standard of education was so low that it had to create ***"sub-standard schools,"* (p.269).** As she ponders on this, she thinks about the fate of her friend Emma. Joanne attempts to make contact with Emma, but does not succeed. Joanne, like the rest of the migrant Grenadians, had come to realize that ***"we had all been deluded into the belief that everything in the "garden" called England was rosy:"* (p.269)** especially their childish role-playing and high expectations of life in England. Joan states, such high expectations of England were ***"farcical, but we could not have known it – no one could, children or adults,"* (p.269).** Joanne settles down to her ***"English home"*** and comes to terms with the fact that the word ***"home"*** had taken on a new meaning; that of learning about life in Britain and its environs.

She narrates how having made friends, they sought to enjoy their life in England and as young people; they set about exploring and ***"venturing into other parts of the country"* (p.269)** they knew little of. As Joanne grows, her circle of friends widens and one summer a small group of them – all migrant children - decide to go to the South West England or the *West Country* on holiday. They encounter both overt and subtle forms of racism trying to hire a caravan and also experience people's reaction to their colour, while in the West Country. The various dialogues Joanne and members of their holiday group have with the staff hiring caravans; confirm that attempts are being made to prevent them from hiring the caravans.

There are open, racist comments about foreigners from the Caravan Hirers. Joanne's group is given defective caravans and in a battle of wits, protests and defiance, they get what they'd requested in the first place. Joanne talks of the ***"discriminations and prejudices"* (p.285)** that was discussed among her group afterwards and the various contrasting points of views each member of the group expressed, based on their life experiences in England.

Analysis

Joanne has become more vocal as is evident from her interaction with her friends. Her tone is now less critical of England and as time passes, there is less hankering for Grenada. She is learning about England, the people, food or cuisine and landscape and there is a sense that Joanne has now accepted England as ***"home."*** This brings us back to the notion of ***"distancing"*** as we saw with the Grenadians when they were leaving the island – physical distance engenders mental/emotional distancing also. Both Aunty Mary and Irene are now ***"distant"*** from the Caribbean in geographical and cultural terms. However, their level of assimilation into the British culture appears to be minimal and this is unhelpful to Joanne. She is asked to prepare a **High Tea** menu for her school cookery homework and is at a loss as to where to begin.

We learn that to lack knowledge of your immediate environment, causes disappointment and a feeling of ***defeat.*** Joanne says that the ***"ceded defeat in the homework department with my Cookery teacher" (p.268)*** as she does not know what a **High Tea** is, neither does her mother nor her aunt. This is quite significant, as Joanne who has recently arrived in England, has just entered her very first school and is being asked to prepare a menu that originated from the eighteenth and nineteenth centuries among the upper classes in Britain. Not only would she not have been acquainted with the culture of the place, but the English cuisine would have been quite new to Joanne also. But should such a situation be the reason to **"brand"** her as **Educationally Sub-Normal**?

Commonly called ***Afternoon Tea,*** a **High Tea** was largely a social event for the upper classes. The drinking of tea not only became a social event for the upper classes, it altered the time and manner in which they took tea. It was a meal that could be eaten when their servants were away or not available. The upper class **'High Tea'** involved a range of teas that can vary from half a dozen to over a hundred varieties; including some very rare and obscure ones.

Nowadays, depending on where you choose to have a **High Tea**, some of the top hotels in London would charge you £35 per person for this meal which could include champagne, a selection of freshly prepared finger sandwiches; warm scones with clotted cream and preserves and a variety of home-made cakes and pastries. With the range of teas could be added pigeon, veal, salmon and fruit.

A **High Tea** is therefore an English meal associated with class differences and it transpires that this did not appear to be of importance to the migrants since, ***"one of the greatest ambitions of Caribbean nationals in England was to be able to buy their own home in England," (p.268).*** For them the notion of ***"destiny"*** is tied with accumulating wealth, which Joanne tells us is seen as ***"the envy of some, since it accorded them respect, power, rank and a rite-de-passage to success apart from book learning," (p.268).*** It therefore means that the idea of ***success and destiny*** means different things to different age groups.

However, we can agree that migrants' real fear of their children being sent to **Educationally Sub-Normal Schools** was not baseless. Historically, one teacher who had first-hand knowledge of this system of education was Bernard Coard, a Grenadian teacher of the 1970's, before he became Deputy Prime Minister of Grenada during the time of Maurice Bishop's New Jewel Party. Coard states that, ***"The schools were being utilized by the education Authorities as a dumping ground for black children. This was especially so for those who had recently come from the Caribbean to join their parents; often after a separation of several years. These children were therefore encountering various degrees of emotional disturbance; on top of the normal cultural and other adjustment problems associated with a sudden move to an entirely new environment,"***[2] Therefore, Joanne's lack of knowledge of a **High Tea** could have been considered a risk factor that would have branded her *as educationally sub-normal* and sent to an **ESN** school. Coard states, ***"The response of the Authorities was not one of addressing their difficulties and needs, but of branding many of them as "educationally subnormal," and then dispatching them to ESN schools."***[2]

Historically, the educational and cultural context of migrants' children during the early 1970's, finding themselves in the English environment *adjusting* to the culture, means that they ran the real risk of being **branded** as *educationally sub-normal*. Joanne was lucky to have escaped this fate. However, Jessica, another Grenadian girl, the narrator tells us, became a victim of this system and ended up being sent to an **ESN** school.

To overcome such stigmatism, notice that it is the children of the migrant parents who are bent on exploring England because they realize they ***"had only lived in one sector of the community,"* decided to *"venture into other parts of the country,"* (p.269).** Many of these children had ***"lived all of their lives"* (p.269)** in England, meaning that some of them were born there and their intention is therefore to ***"enjoy our home"* (p.269).** Adults, it seems, were too busy working, surviving and congregating in ***"one sector of the community,"* (p.269)** to assimilate.

As Joanne relates hers and the group's experiences, she has become ***"perceptive"*** with a mature tone and assertive language that shows her developing confidence. What we see of their interaction with the Caravan Hire Company is reflective of Irene's own experience with the General Assistants in her workplace. Superficially, there is communication which is tolerant between the two groups but the undercurrent is that of racism. Joanne comments that, ***"There was a broad and tolerant atmosphere"* (p.280)** between the group and the Hiring Staff. However, overt racism is presented glibly by talking about another race, despite the fact that Mr. Stuart is talking to Joanne's and her friends, who are a foreign group anyway!

There is a sense here that Mr. Stuart's is suggesting 'I really don't mind you but I don't like the others.' In this psychological game-playing, Mr. Stuart makes it clear that he is ***"Not keen on foreigners,"* (p.279)** and is overtly racist when he says of Indians, ***"Don't like Indians at all."*** Despite the fact that he pretended that Joanne's group was acceptable, his actions produced a sting in the tail; he deliberately gives them defective vehicles that could risk all their lives; they lose 2 days out of their planned holiday, having to wait for the weekend to tackle Mr. Stuart, who clearly was not remorseful. Joanne says it was, ***"a strange undertaking indeed – this reckless, incredible event, full***

of blatant and discrimination prejudices, stemming from ignorance of the worst kind!" (p.285).

At the end of this Chapter, the image of the children battling for their rights with Mr. Stuart and ***"the guv'nor"*** is riddled with pathos. There is similarity here with what the Grenadian adults in the novel had experienced, especially Calvin, Irene, Byron, and to some extent Aunty Mary. It also confirms the details of the children's discussion that life in ***England was not easy*** as well as the Grenadian children's discussion that the migrants in England were having a difficult time there.

We therefore empathise with Joanne when she tells us that some, or the entire group had ***"faced such experiences before and would encounter again," (p.285).*** This suggests that it is the prevailing social situation or the status quo and one that impacts adversely on other areas of life. Joanne says the experience ***"had been such a mental strain, so powerful that throughout the holiday, it had brought hasty exchange of angry words and anxiety between the group for the well-being and safe return of the vans," (p.285).*** This takes us back to Calvin and Irene's domestic situation and perhaps enables us to understand the impact of his experiences as ***"a Black man"*** on his mentality and ability to provide for his family. It evidences that external stimuli has an impact on the internal workings of relations within the domestic/group situations. Joan concludes that, ***"the colour of our skin, our only crime," (p.286).*** This fact of life for the migrants in Britain appears to cause tensions that underpin **Part II** of the novel's plot, characterization, and themes.

The theme of ***racial prejudice*** in this Chapter, as well as the previous Chapter, is presented as a universal theme of people's intolerance of others. In the novel there are two instances of racial prejudice (the encounter of the group of Grenadian children with the Caravan Hiring Company and Irene and the General Assistants in her work-place). This is used to show an example of people's complex inhumanity to others and how this impacts on the wider circles of their lives. Located in **Part II** of the novel; where there is interaction between the British and ***"foreigners,"*** it shows these instances of prejudice as the real antagonist of those who are enlightened. Neither of these instances dominate the novel, but are interwoven structurally to complement characterization, especially Calvin, Irene, Peter, perhaps Darris and Byron, in **Part II** of the novel.

CHAPTER 13 – SUMMARY & ANALYSIS

CHARACTERS	RELATIONSHIPS
Joanne	**Narrator in England**
Irene	**Joanne's mother**
Darris & Darrin	**Joanne's twin sisters**
Tony	**Darris' boyfriend**
Aunty Mary	**Irene's sister and Joanne's aunt**

Events in the Novel

1. Joanne and her friends continue to travel around England's West Country, as the landscape there reminds them of Grenada. They attempt to imitate Grenadian lifestyle but the West Country does not provide the right atmosphere.
2. Joanne's twin sisters leave their home; Darris goes to live with her English boyfriend and Darrin leaves to become a Christian Missionary in Africa. They leave Joanne at home with their mother.
3. Irene is heartbroken and she tries to cope with this by becoming so obsessive with work that she collapses at work and is taken to hospital.
4. Joanne is never told about Randolph in the 19 years that she has grown up with her mother. She becomes so disappointed that she aborts any attempt to rekindle her mother and father's relationship or searching for Randolph.
5. Despite Joanne's urgent need of help and support from the twins to look after their mother, the twins abandon Joanne.
6. Irene remains in hospital where she ignores Joanne and instead calls for the twins who are not interested anyway. Joanne remains steadfast in her support of her mother until her suspicion that she was being used conveniently is confirmed.
7. Joanne is comforted by Gran-gran's past advice and guidance, and recognizes that she has some of the characteristics of becoming ***"A Woman of Destiny."***
8. Joanne is very angry that she has to face her mother's death alone; since it is one of society's tabooed subject alone, as there are no Handbooks on how to cope with death and bereavement which she sees as the ***"world's greatest secret"*** **(p.361)**.

Chapter Summary

Joanne and her friends continue to travel around England's West Country, specifically as the green landscape reminds them of Grenada. There is an attempt to recreate experiences that are similar to those in the Grenadian environment – green landscape; narrow country lanes, with matted, stubbly bush on either side, being able to see the starry sky at night; enjoying the darkness of the nights and mock-storytelling.

Joanne's twin sisters are now grown up and Darris has a white English boyfriend. He is a 21 years old boy from the North of England. Irene is not impressed and does not think he is a right match for Darris for a number of reasons: he does not have a family to present to him; she disapproves of their late party-going; the fact that Tony is white is an ***"unknown quantity"* (p.292)** to Irene; Tony living in a Council flat and of Darris going to live with Tony before marriage; she therefore feels his intentions are not genuine.

Irene's views seem rather old-fashioned to the youngsters. Their kind of independence of mind and spirit, having a job, their own money, wanting to live on their own without the marriage commitment, just did not seem to square with Irene. Irene, it seems, was looking forward to a white wedding, obvious by her secret little wedding purchases over time. Additionally, her twin sister Darrin is also skeptical of Tony.

The planned move out of Irene's home draws closer and Irene's anxiety forces her to tell Darris of a miscarriage she suffered as well as the catalogue of things which had gone wrong in her life as follows: A ***"Doctor's misdiagnosis"* (p.292),** having had birth-control in place and tales of woe about people she had known, who had suffered a similar fate. She blames these on deliberate racism with a sinister intention to prevent black women from ***"populating Britain with lots of little black bastard children,"* (p.292).** Darris feels her mother has become paranoid but Irene's retort is, ***"only those whose backside are in the fire, know how hot it is!"* (p.292)**

Irene's disappointment has much to do with wanting to show Calvin that she had done well without his help as a father. Irene has never spoken about her relationship with Randolph, who continued to exist in Joanne's mind as a shadowy ghost. Joanne realizes that adults like Irene play ***"hate till death"* (p.294)** games which are in stark contrast to children's nature to instantly forgive.

Irene has never broached the subject about Randolph to Joanne over the past 19 years, and she happily continues as if he did not exist. Joanne concludes that it is an existence of double standards ***"Jekyll and Hyde"* (p.295)** and one she will be careful to avoid in the future. As a result, Joanne questions whether the details in Irene's letters to Aunt Meena about Randolph and his family were true. Therefore, without an opposite view or alternative input to make comparisons, Joanne feels that matters are probably best left alone.

Joanne appears to have an epiphany the moment she decides not to bother with the Irene-Randolph scenario. She expresses her decision to break with the, ***"wilderness, in search of tender care,"* (p.295)** as rejuvenating. She says that relinquishing the need to go and seek answers gave her a sense of freedom; gave her a feeling of having achieved adulthood; made her a teller of her own tale and master of her own life.

In the meantime, Darris leaves home and cohabits with Tony. Her twin sister becomes involved in church activities and sets her sights on becoming a missionary. The girls' exit from Irene's nest, took its toll on her health, and Irene's resolve weakens by their absence. Irene becomes a workaholic to compensate for her sense of failure and loss. Aunt Mary's visits lessen and the domestic nest is empty, ***"bereft of excitement and laughter and anticipation of good things,"* (p.296).**

Irene collapses at work from exhaustion one day and has two heart attacks within 24hr and Joanne is called to the hospital where she is taken. Irene does not acknowledges Joanne but instead asks for the twins and goes back to sleep. Joanne feels the rejection, now more acute that her presence in this ***"moment of crisis*" (p.299)** is of no consequence. This was not the first occasion as Joanne says that it is ***"what I had long held as my existence of convenience,*" (p.299).** Feeling used and abused, Joanne is quite shaken by the experience of being by-passed and she resurrects from this emotional wound by reflecting on Gran-gran's ***"advice and personal words of comfort, just as I had held on to the three beads she had given me,*" (p.299).**

Joanne's tone is reflective of the characteristics that Gran-gran outlined in her parting farewell from Grenada. She is ***"inspired to accept what to others seemed unacceptable;"* (p.299).** Joanne now has ***"visions and goals and aims thought impossible to achieve by others,*"** and she is now has ***"inexplicable strength, unshakeable determination to get ahead and an unwavering drive to accomplish Gran-gran's long term goals for her life,"* (p.299).**

Joanne is emerging as ***"A Woman of Destiny,"*** as outlined by Gran-gran and she deals with the impact of her twin sisters' non-involvement in their mother's care as ***"a solitary bearing of burden and isolation,* (p.300)."** Darrin has moved to Birmingham and Darris to Africa as a Christian missionary. Joanne is left to cope with the ***"fatigue, anger and frustration*" (p.300)** as she compares the possibility of being in a similar situation in Grenada, where there would be as a matter of course a network of support from the folks. She is concerned about how she will cope with her mother's death and feels inadequate to deal with the enormity of bereavement; a subject she feels society does not prepare individuals for. Joanne sees this as ***"society's conspiracy to force individuals to experience extreme trauma at a time when knowledge of coping strategies could minimize that pain,"* (p301).** Joanne is very angry that she has to face the ***"world's greatest secret*" (p.301)** alone. There is a poignant reminder that it is glossed over, made euphemistically to seem ***"more palatable, was mainly associated with the after-shocks and counseling,*" (p.301).** She gets home exhausted and sleeps for 12 hours still fully clothed in her work clothes.

Analysis

This final Chapter presents Joanne as an adult who has a good deal to say about the complexities of life. She has become very pragmatic about her role as a daughter and projects a strong sense of what she will tolerate in her life; one of Gran-gran's requisite characteristics Gran-gran of being *"A Woman of Destiny."*

This Chapter also presents an interesting dilemma about *landscape* and individual attitudes to it. The whole notion of *landscape* is an interesting one, as we learn that Joanne and her friends continue to visit South West England because '*The West Country*' reminds them of Grenada. In other words, we see the group's attempts to recreate their Grenadian experience because the Cornish landscape is akin to Grenada more than any other place; its green and hilly, has thick darkness at nights, narrow country lanes and matted bush, starry skies at night, but not quite conducive to the kind of storytelling sessions they have been used to in Grenada. However, Cornwall as a place sufficed but on a deeper level, this behaviour is typical of diasporic communities' need to recreate their cultural identity wherever they are located or 'transplanted'.

Interesting in this final Chapter, is also the different perspectives of how the word *landscape* can be interpreted; based on the *nationality* of the migrants and their children. There are at least 3 different ways of interpreting the notion of *landscape* here: *a mental construct or state of mind*; *physical landscape known as "back home*" and *cultural representation.*

Firstly, the attempt to recreate Grenada is signified here as *'a state of mind'* rather than an actual place. This is so for many exiles or migrants and their children who left Grenada to join their parents in England. We see this in this final Chapter, among *Joanne and her friends,* who attempt to recreate aspects of Grenada's social landscape in the West Country. It means that Grenada remains in them as a *'mental construct'* where the imagery is nostalgic and is seen as 'perfect.' Joanne also projected this view in **Chapter 9**, after first arriving in England, when she complained bitterly about the *"sameness"* of England and regretted having left Grenada.

Secondly, migrants such as *Aunty Mary, Irene, Calvin, Byron, Manny, Velma* and those who have migrated to England from Grenada, with a prolonged absence from the region (including *Manny* from Jamaica); England has become a resident *"home."* This group would ultimately refer to the *physical Grenadian landscape* as *"back home."* For many of them, Grenada is a place where they would retire to, when they no longer wish to remain in the Diaspora or the place that they elect to be their final resting place, for their interred remains. *Irene* falls in this latter category, when Joanne carries out her wish to be buried *under the silk cotton tree* in Grenada: (Seen in both the **Prologue** and **Epilogue**).

Thirdly, the children who were born in England of migrant parents, for them the most important **meaning attached to the Grenadian landscape** is *cultural representation*. It has to do with what they regard their *cultural identity* to be. Having been born of Caribbean parents in England, there is therefore creation of a *new identity* based on a **fusion** of a common historical background i.e., particular ways of representing Grenadian culture (e.g. via language, food, music; psychological levels of thinking and discourse) and *culturally mixed ideologies* – (those with **both British and Grenadian backgrounds**). *Darris, Darrin and Peter* falls into this category.

As we come to the end of the *narration/song,* Irene emerges here as someone who has certain standards she wants her daughters to project and we see her criticizing her daughter's choice of a partner. She is not happy the fact that Tony's family is not involved in decision-making in his life and questions the quality of his lifestyle; living in a Council flat and going out to parties after 10.30pm. She relates what she regards being *"decent"* means by her criticism of the following: a person's manner of dress, wanting to give the right impression to others, waiting to be married before living together, and choosing a non-white partner; all of which Darris concluded is a form of "paranoia" and her mother being out of touch with modern society. In contrast, Aunty Mary is presented as someone who is more consolatory, tolerant of the new generation's style of living and compromises with the differences between Grenada and England. Aunty Mary seems to have assimilated more into the British way of life compared to Irene and though she seems to say little, she is still influential in her silence and quiet manner of dealing with issues.

Another noteworthy point in this Chapter is Irene's recount to Darris of a past miscarriage she suffered. This tale was told to Darris when Irene realized the girl was hell-bent on leaving the household to live with Tony. This episode is reflective of Gran-gran's recount of her rape by Mr. McDonald, when Gran-gran had realized that Joanne was definitely leaving for England. Both Irene and Gran-gran's reasons were to instill caution into the girls by their 'shock' tactics, as a folk story-telling approach to teaching them good sense.

This Chapter also holds the key as to why Joanne aborts her quest to find her father. We see a disappointed Joanne, who feels she has waited long enough for matters to be revealed to her by her mother. There is a sense that Irene's reaction to the Darris choice opened the psychological cracks in Irene's life that she had cleverly concealed. Joanne tells us that Irene seemed ***"weak and conquered by Darris' episode,"*** **(p.293).** This enabled her to reflect on Irene as a person in less emotional terms. Joanne is able to dissect and unravel the issues surrounding her life and the absence of her father by looking at Irene's character.

What we are told is significant as Joanne now realizes that her ***"past childhood wonderings about my entry into the word was never fulfilled,"*** **(p.293).** There is disappointment that Irene has never ever spoken to Joanne about her past and Joanne concludes that her birth was a "non-event." Joanne takes us back to the belief by the folks that ***"children must be seen and not heard,"*** **(p.16)** as something that is not innate in them, despite the location, even though they had ***"crossed the Atlantic Ocean from Grenada to England, still demanding silence from the young when it was convenient,"*** **(p.293).**

It is a criticism on the cultural practices because Joanne, the adult, is able to analyse life decisions in more realistic terms. She has come to the conclusion that adults play games against each other, and she says of Irene that, ***"she was hell bent on showing the estranged father, how well she had done without his help in bringing up her girls,"*** **(p.293).** There is a suggestion that there is *revenge* involved in Irene's actions; the underlying reasons for bringing up the girls is based on ***"showing the estranged father"*** **(p.293)** her super capabilities.

In dissecting the issues further, Joanne realizes now that she is older and is able to reason as an adult. She concludes that what she had learnt from Aunt Meena's letters were one-sided information and could not be taken at face-value, based on her real life experiences of living with Irene. She realizes that her ***"inquisitive appetite, which echoed and re-***

***echoed during times of stress, feelings of self-pity and sadness*" (p.293)** had perhaps exaggerated her sense of **"*loss*"** for the **"*missing piece of jigsaw,*" (p.294).** As she analyses the psychology of her situation, she concludes that the attitude of **"*hate-till-death*" (p.294)** is an adult game compared with children's ease of forgiveness and though for her **"*time had tempered the many years of wishful thinking,*" (p.294)** it had not done so for her mother Irene. She makes a profound statement when she decides finally that she would learn from **"*the realities of what's seen and experienced,*" (p.294).** In other words, she would look at the hard facts, based on the possibility that Randolph's life could now present a complex scenario; linked with a family of his own. At this point, Joanne has come to realize that her longings, desires and projected imaginings of a happy ending based on the **"*life-long wish for mummy-Randolph scenario*" (p.294)** to be rekindled, was perhaps not achievable.

It was at her mother's deathbed, **"*something in mum's eyes caused that firmly rooted feeling to shake,*" (p.299).** Joanne finally accepts she has truly been abandoned, **"*by the feeling of abandonment…an uncanny sense of unease,*" (p.299)** and there is perhaps a deeper sense of being abandoned by both her mother and father. There is disappointment in Joanne's voice as she makes a final decision not to pursue the quest. This is evident in the criticism of her own part played in her journey to discovery. She questions her intention for the first time when she wonders whether it was, **"*the depravation of the mind to offer an alternative jib-saw piece where nothing existed,*" (p.295).**

We feel a sense of disappointment for the experienced, adult Joanne, who is now able to overcome her **"*childish passion*"** and realises that **"*life had been complicated ….and maybe best left alone to unravel its mysteries in the fullness of time,*" (p.295).** Despite not achieving her stated objective to find her father, there is a sense that Joanne has become pragmatic and her decision to curtail the quest is not a weakness, rather a strength which confirms Gran-gran's characteristics of being **"*A Woman of Destiny.*"** These are as follows:

1. Joanne demonstrates **strength** of character and is able to look at life and come to decisions that best suit her, rather than pursue 'meaningless' dreams.

2. Joanne remains **steadfast** and **unchanging** in her quest for knowledge, the truth of her existence and demonstrates **staying power** by her consistency at self-development.

3. Joanne is **not easily suppressed**; we see this with her reaction to Justin's dad's comments about her abilities and possible future. We also see this in her determination to be educated and explore England and the role played among her friends in England and in this Chapter, her determination to soldier on.

4. Joanne demonstrates a **tenacity** or thirst for knowledge, clearly seen in her school days in England, described as **"*a passion,*" (p.267)** but also seen here in the last Chapter as someone who will challenge or fight for her right.

5. Joanne is **pragmatic**, she learns from her experience, is able to dissect and analyse issues and come to decisions, based on those without unrealistic or emotional attachments.

6. Throughout the novel, we see Joanne's use of **memory and actively remembering** as qualities which enabled her to overcome many situations: especially when she felt deeply wounded by her mother's rejection of her**: *"Gran-gran had taught me to be strong at all times and I had held on to her advice and personal words of comfort, just as I had held on to the three beads she had given me,"* (p.299).** Therefore, whether we agree that she holds these qualities or not, Joanne herself categorically states the impact on her life.

7. The use she makes of **point of contact with the beads** she tells us, ***"They inspired me to accept what to others seemed unacceptable, held visions of goals and aims thought impossible to achieve by others. Above all, they had bought a sense of inexplicable strength, unshakeable determination to get ahead and an unwavering drive to accomplish Gran-gran's long-term goals for my life – to get to the top, no matter what!"* (p.299)**

However, though somewhat apprehensive about coping with her mother's death and bereavement, we can be confident that, invested with the qualities of being ***a woman of destiny,*** Joanne will be able to cope **and *"respond to life's most inevitable event,"* (p.302).**

Epilogue

We return to the cemetery, where Joanne is standing under the silk cotton tree in the **Prologue**. The funeral attendees have left the graveside and Joanne remains by the grave and uses quietude to reflect and come to terms with the death of a mother she realizes was ***"a stranger in many ways,"* (p.304).** In fact, Joanne is ***"stupefied by unpalatable revelations about mum's own private world,"* (p.304),** as she relates the ***"web of deception"* (p.305)** she had unearthed after her mother died.

The **Epilogue** confirms what Joanne has already felt in the novel's last Chapter, when she says she experienced with Irene, ***"the feeling of abandonment…an uncanny sense of unease,"* (p.299).** This is now borne out in what Joanne learns later that ***"stupefies"*** her. We learn that Irene's character was the embodiment of ***"hate of an extraordinary kind,"* (p.304)** evident by her complex psychology which harboured bitterness, secrecy, a lifetime of woes, deliberate destruction of Joanne's past relationships with Emma, past boyfriends, by not passing on letters that they had all written to Joanne, and the most important, withholding information about Randolph, by hiding all his letters from America to her.

Additionally, Irene had deliberately left Joanne out of her **Will** and instead, gave everything to the twins; Joanne's job application replies with offers of jobs were also withheld from her; and Irene had daubed Joanne ***"the niece"* (p.308)**, to past working colleagues. In other words, she disowned her as a daughter. This is an act of betrayal, Joanne says, ***"cut through her heart like the repeated stabbing of an uncured wound, causing fresh bleeding at each attack,"* (p.305).** In other words, each act of betrayal Joanne uncovered violated the implicit promise of love and protection, (between mother and daughter) that also gives a child the courage to love others.

The imagery of violence, evident by the language Joanne uses to describe her reaction to the revelations, suggests the intensity and impact of this on her psyche. Therefore, being ***"wounded"* (p.305)** is an expression of the psychological/emotional pain Joanne felt. This pain was made extreme by the fact that Joanne realizes that Irene's resentment and anger at Randolph was used to punish her; not so much for doing something wrong but for her painful reflections in the mirror of love. Irene it seems had psychologically attacked Joanne because she did not like the reflection of Randolph that Joanne's existence represents.

There is no doubt that Irene herself has experienced a form of intimate betrayal by Randolph. Her coping strategy was manifested in both the physical and emotional 'locking away' of the memory/letters from Randolph in the little ***"grip"*** she travelled from Grenada to England with. Such motivation we can conclude, gave Irene a feeling of empowerment; having felt disempowered in her personal relationships with, not only Randolph but later also Calvin. It is possible that this made Irene violate deeper values such as caring about the emotional well-being of her child; in ways that could be both conscious and unconscious at the same time. What is more obvious here is that whatever form Irene's betrayal takes, we can see that it has increased in intensity over time and her damaged psyche was not given an opportunity to heal.

For Joanne, it was important to comprehend all the issues, in order to make sense of it so that the healing process can begin. She questions Aunty Mary who was able to fill in the details and background to her discovery. As usual, Aunty Mary ***tells it like is,*** and Joanne it seems, would have an opportunity to heal as she comes face-to-face with the facts. In contrast, Irene's shame and suffering has been the backdrop to her bitterness, because she did not come to terms with the fact that, ***"people took advantage of that and ridiculed"* (p.306)** their family. We learn from Aunty Mary that the, ***"pressure on individuals causes them to make mistakes, not on purpose but people move where pressure is greatest,"* (p.307).**

Certainly, hurtful episodes do more than just hurt; they are usually accompanied by other emotions including fear, sadness, anger, anxiety, and shame; all which confirm Irene's life experiences to the end of her life. We know that Randolph's parents were instrumental in initiating the separation between the two lovers but Joanne the child, had readily forgiven them believing, as she has discovered, that Randolph actually wanted her. It was important for Joanne to understand that she was not rejected and therefore she will be in a better position to heal and as she deals with past disappointments. As a result, Joanne will be able to project a positive sense of self, as both loveable and acceptable to others.

Joanne's quest has been a journey of self-discovery and the moment she becomes clear about all the issues involved, she experiences an epiphany; a sense of enlightenment that ***restores*** her. She is convinced that all will be well and leaves the cemetery to return to England in order **"*to construct my future*," (p.309).** As she walks away, Joanne tells us that ***physically***, she does not look back; ***symbolically and emotionally***, she puts the past firmly behind her because, **"*The search was over and life had come to another juncture,*" (p.309).** Joanne tells us that she has become an independent thinker who can move on; firmly invested with the qualities that Gran-gran had advised her would be needed to become for her, as well as for the folks, ***A Woman of Destiny***.

FOR ADVANCED STUDIES

Given the scope of this section, it is not possible to explore all of the themes and concepts presented within the novel here. Therefore, Advance Readers should read with an open mind, and tackle explicit and implicit meanings of ideas and themes as they explore the relationship between the Author's intentions and their own interpretations.

CRITICAL INTERPRETATIONS & APPROACHES TO READING

When reading ***A Woman of Destiny***, it is possible to read the events of the story through a literal or a figurative point of view or a combination of the two. One interesting approach is to view the text as a straightforward commentary of childhood; the ***Bildungsroman***. The Author has set this young protagonist on a quest. What happens to her can be viewed as an experiment whereby her innocence and status as a child are abruptly replaced by the harsh realities of a more adult world and she makes her own decision as to whether to continue the quest or not.

Therefore, on one hand, the novel is about the story of a young girl's determination to succeed, despite many obstacles that create a variety of complex, emotional highs and lows; she emerges as a self-directed, independent thinker, positive towards her future goals and very much the teller of her own tale. On the other hand, the novel also offers new interpretation of the characters, events, tackles explicit and implicit meanings of themes and ideas; in ways which lend other types of reading of the novel.

When Joanne leaves Grenada for England, she sees the Authority and power in the Grenadian family's domestic situation that she is used to, as having been removed in England, and she does not take pleasure in this. As the novel progresses, she gradually asserts her independence and expresses mature views, through different power models – truth and lies, inter-generational viewpoints, as well as negative and positive life experiences. Advance Readers might also want to explore the wider issues of gender that the novel is concerned with. For example, questions to consider might be as follows:

- Why are there more females "fathering" children?
- What factors contribute to the men's absence in the children's lives?
- What are the causes that contribute to the men's unfulfilled destinies?
- Why is there a lack of positive involvement or role-modeling among the males who have not travelled?
- What does the lack of a positive ***Destiny*** imply about the men's ability to function in the traditional society?
- What is the relationship between 'cultural/traditional' upbringing and vestiges of colonialism in the novel?
- Is Thompson's story a cautionary tale about behaviour that perpetuates and replicates, as well as issues to do with male functionality in the home/society?

Advanced Readers should be prepared to undertake independent reading of related genres and critical theories which may inform their interpretation of the text.

A Psychoanalytic Approach

It may be that characters in the novel represent each aspect of the personality. From this we may look at [5]Freud's concept of the 'psyche;' the individual personality. Freud believed that the psyche is made up of three parts:

(1). The **id,** which is concerned with our basic needs and desires.
(2). The **superego,** is centered on the normal aspirations and prohibitions.
(3). The **ego,** is concerned with striking a balance between the **id** and the **superego**.

However, the fact that Joanne never gains complete power over her desires and outcome, may suggest that bowing to our basic desires can sometimes be dangerous and unsatisfactory. Joanne represents the **id**. Gran-gran represents the **superego,** as she worries about the goals to achieve in becoming the *Woman of Destiny*; as well as the orders and rules for achieving this. The reader needs to question why Joanne gives up the quest and destroys our expectation of its outcome. The **Metaphorical ego**, represented by Aunty Mary, maintains cohesion among the migrant group, as she is the driving force that seeks compromise among them in England.

Additionally, the change of viewpoint in the end of the novel, of Joanne not wanting to pursue her quest, defies the characteristic expectation that *'things will turn out right in the end.'* The fact is, Joanne demonstrates that things don't always turn out right, and therefore the fairytale ending is denied. The presumptions of the **id-like** fairytale or imagined outcomes were not secure and have, as a result, become fragmented. Therefore, having been greatly disappointed by the mother, the reader may want to question whether Joanne's desires for a father-daughter relationship have really been quenched. Is this narrative open to endless interpretations and modern adaptations? An Advanced Reader may also want to expand discussion on the role of *Memory* in the text, as discussed on page 54 of this Study Guide.

History & the Literary Narrative

According to post-modernist thinkers, history is a system or a narrative which should be challenged. Such thinkers claim that there is no absolute truth and that the way people perceive the world is subjective or personal. [5]Michel Foucault sees history as only interpretation of interpretation. In other words, he believes that the history we are given is fictional and we should be suspicious of it. In *A Woman of Destiny,* we learn about various historical aspects of the characters' lives which are also embodied in recorded historical data which relate to Grenada, (and the wider Caribbean), Britain, France and the USA. Therefore, is *A Woman of Destiny* providing an alternative history via the "***diasporic narrative***," which subverts the notion of betterment elsewhere; for those who once viewed their existence as somewhat dystopian? There is a sense that the mythical is subverted as the story comes to a close; because chasing the existence of *Eldorado* in England proved to be a misconception. The Advanced Reader may want to interrogate the notion of alternative history presented, especially the subjective views of characters, their initial certainties or assumptions and the reality of their experiences.

Post-Modernism

Post-modernism is an interrogation of the individual's place in society. ***A Woman of Destiny*** presents a world in which a quest results in the collapse of expectation and becomes inverted. However, ideas which are central to the concept of post-modernism are characterized by the crisis of realization. This crisis is evident in ***A Woman of Destiny*** by rejection, from the result of assumed certainty of efforts and present reality.

Post-modernism suggests that apparent realities are only social constructs which are subject to change as the individuals change. As such, it implies that the individual is at risk of losing a defined subjective position when faced with the crisis of realization e.g. Justin's dad, Irene, Jessica, Calvin, the youth in England. They present views of themselves versus that of others. As a result, what constitutes the individual has a tendency to become fragmented when conditions change and this can be seen in confrontations with Justin's dad, Calvin, Byron, Irene, and Jessica in the novel. Therefore, the Advanced Reader may want to expand on the notion of post-modernism as an interrogation of what constitutes reality and how an individual sees himself engaged in that reality within society.

Genderised Boundaries and the Self

A possible reading of the text ***A Woman of Destiny*** is that from one point of view, it highlights the futility of the woman's fight on her own without the male input. On the other hand, it demonstrates the women's fortitude, defiance and strength of characters in going it alone. However, the boundaries between the self and 'self' as a social construct can be seen in the projected views of what the notion of ***Destiny*** entails in the novel. Other boundaries are between the church and society; male vs. female; immigrants vs. host society, and one's own tradition and culture vs adaptation to other cultures. Irene's sense of self, versus the social idea of how successful she is as a person, is tied up with what she personally feels and the dominant view of what others think of her. These are binary oppositions that wrestle with her sense of achievement. Therefore, we witness the consequence of this as a divided self, with a pathology that has an underlying psychosis, characterized by destruction.

Similarly, for the protagonist, her deepest desires are revealed, exposing her to a self-knowledge that she has little help with. Therefore, the reality of trauma is something that the Author interrogates through behaviour. From the various perspectives on behaviour, we get a glimpse of what society can be, without the veneer of pretence and unrealistic impositions of expectations that are meant to 'drive' the characters.

However, in Joanne's character, it seems likely that the Author is directly alluding to the terrifying aspects of migration of children from Grenada/Caribbean, and specifically its impact on the psyche of those branded ***"educationally subnormal.*"** For those who were identified as such, their sense of identity would be one of rejection, the fact they were seen as '*sub-standard*;' meaning, not quite meeting the required levels of acceptance or criteria for being regarded as '*normal*.' Life in the two landscapes provided a catalyzing process for the characters; whether via various occasions and events e.g. traditional cultures, schooling, employment, holidaying, or domestic difficulties. These have subsequently proved to be challenging, defeating, successful for some, inconclusive for others; and have also influenced their sense of self and cultural identification/allegiance. Through this, the Author is perhaps suggesting that the conditions under which identity is traditionally understood are unstable, and is dependent on interactions between individuals within a group. As a result, the social assumptions that constitutes or identifies the individual, is likely to be affected when conditions change.

A Symbolic Approach

Alternatively, ***A Woman of Destiny*** can be read more figuratively. The journey to self-discovery could simply be a device that the Author used to make a wider and far more troubling comment on society. This can be seen via the many events and innocent wanderings of the children. For e.g. the girls' discovery of their periods and their inability to cope with it; a lack of clear information on how to manage relationships with boys; adult child-rearing approaches of deliberately leaving children in ignorance as a survival strategy; the different approaches to bringing-up boys from bringing up girls; excessive physical punishment; the lasting effects of colonialism on different levels in society; the trauma experienced by struggling relatives who are left to bring up children who are not theirs; inter-generational/racial conflict, and the resulting emergence of a collective consciousness among migrants in a host society; and the factors which engender these.

Symbolically also, it is possible that the absence of positive male role-modeling in the text is meant to suggest a number of readings. For example,

- That a society without male input is unstable or
- That men are to be seen as irresponsible *Don Juans* who shirk their responsibilities, leaving women to do all or
- Men projected as a major influence in society, who might offer protection and love to females and children but achievable through compromise instead of competition.

Colonialism, Education and Migration

The 20th century was a period in which Administrators of the European Empires believed that it was their mission to conquer and civilize parts of the globe. Simultaneously, European literature and historical studies of the colonial period tended to assume superiority of Western civilization and life in the West, over that of colonized peoples and their cultures. As a result, the subjugated peoples in the colonies imbued such perceptions; also believing what they had was inferior to their colonizers. Consequently, there was a hankering for the things of the West, evidenced by imitative Western styles, and a longing to live in the West. The popular thinking was that to advance in life, one needed to be in such environments. This is coupled with the fact that economically, those migrating to the West had a better chance of improving their lot in life quickly. This perpetuated the view that Western countries' colonizing mission to govern, educate and develop other people's culture was for the people's own good. However, such ideas were challenged during the post World War II era, on several fronts:

(1). In movements calling for freedom from Western rule
(2). Countries seeking independence from Western dominance
(3). The emergence of academic fields of post-colonial studies.

Therefore, post-colonial thinking developed as a moral critique of the historical processes of Western colonization since the 16th century. For example, this took the form of interrogating the exploitation of slavery and forced labour, genocide of indigenous peoples, and studies of settler societies developed as a result of migration to large cities in Western Europe (especially Britain), Canada and the USA. Such societies have produced "*hybrid*" cultures or '*racialised others,*' which grew up in these rich cities, and at the same time, produced a first and subsequent generations of migrants or 'Diaspora' communities.

Edward Said[6] portrays the corrupting effects of power of the colonizers and dominant cultures through their practice of constructing racialised others who were supposedly childlike and inferior. From the beginning of ***A Woman of Destiny***, themes of colonialism which are clearly visible include Irene, the protagonist's mother, and other Grenadians leaving the island by a passenger ship, bound for England; where they perceive their social and economic status will be better and where believe they will advanced at a faster rate than with life at home. Additionally, the children of such migrants are "*children in waiting,*" as they too are expected to follow in their parents' footsteps to England and USA, with similar expectations e.g. Joanne, Emma and Emery. The protagonist and her best friend actively demonstrate this perception by their role-playing of how they imagined their lives in England would be.

In ***A Woman of Destiny,*** there is an image of superiority, associated with England and the USA, projected as *Eldora do*; a land of abundance, where it is thought "*the streets are paved with gold,* "compared with the migrants' meager existence at home. Throughout the novel, the Author undermines this sense of superiority and colonial notion of '*Britishness*' or '*Englishness*' expressed in the text, seen as:

- The superiority of "books," over traditional/oral culture
- Colonial education and the preferred content of its curriculum voiced by Justin's dad
- Maintaining '*Britishness*' - the role played by those who head education delivery in Grenada e.g. Mr. Jessup, the English headmaster and Mr. Glover, the music teacher
- The religious input from Canadian missionaries who specifically target children in the island

This sense of superiority in culture and lifestyle is undermined by the Author, as we are invited to explore the reality of the Grenadian migrants' experiences via an inversion of the myth. In other words, the migrant's expectation is denied and we see this on a number of occasions throughout the novel. For example, Irene's life is a psychological bungle; Calvin's and Byron's intransigence and confrontation with their employers in refusing to do menial tasks in England and the repercussions of their actions; the disappointments expressed in Irene's letters, compared with previous expectations e.g. to remain in England for only 5 years; difficulties experienced domestically, as well as in coping strategies within the harsh labour-market environment (e.g. Velma and Manny/ Irene and Calvin); Aunty Mary's moments of quiet reflection and regret of their previously held views of England, and the reality of their experiences; the additional information from the children's innocent wanderings about second-hand information they receive about migrants' distressful experiences in England, (as discussed in St. John's river); a first-hand experience and glimpse into Irene's working condition, as well as the migrants' children's experience of racial prejudice, seen when they attempt to hire caravans for a holiday.

The migrants' experiences show that their earlier perceptions about England were misconstrued and therefore wrong in their simple, fairytale expectations, that all will be well there. From this, it is possible to see how the Author has completely undermined the authoritative notion that "*the best is to be found in the West.*" In our brief glimpse of the characters' lives, we are allowed to the see the result of their colonial presumptions, by being forced to see the limitation of these platitudes.

Additionally, the removal of influential adults in the narrator's life in England, from **Part II** of the narrative, is a device used to allow Joanne, the young protagonist, the freedom to evolve with maturity as a *Woman of Destiny*, without adults' influence to pass judgment on her actions. It is also a convenient way of making Joanne demonstrate her own independence and courage, perhaps suggestive of the view that the ingredients which create *destiny*/success lies within, rather than outside of the person, and perhaps not necessarily specific to a particular place.

Reader Response:

Other Points to Consider in the Novel

- **Novel of childhood**
- **Religion/education as colonialism**
- **Post-colonial text**
- **Diaspora text**

Whatever reading perspective is taken in reading ***A Woman of Destiny*** novel, as a reader responding to the text, you will bring your own experiences and knowledge to it, which will also lend other possible forms of interpretations. Enjoy!

Thanks to all our Calypsonians past and present!!

The Mighty Sparrow	Lord Nelson	Sugar Aloes	All Rounder
Mighty Duke	Bro Valentino	Albert M. Gomes	Pink Panther
Mighty Shadow	Black Stalin	Chrystal Beckles	David Rudder
Lord Pretender	Lingo	Tigress Joanne Rowley	Duanne O'Connor
Black Prince	Brother Resistance	De Fosto	Mighty Striker

REFERENCES

1. Michael White, "How the Empire gong could be dumped in the dustbin of history" (interview by Patrick Barkham), *The Guardian*, 14 July 2004.

2. **ESN** (means *Educationally Subnormal*). During the 1970's there was a focus on sending Caribbean children to schools which were labeled ESN schools. *"These schools were previously, officially called schools for the mentally subnormal (MSN). The schools were being utilized by the education Authorities as a dumping ground for black children. This was especially so for those who had recently come from the Caribbean to join their parents; often after a separation of several years. These children were therefore encountering various degrees of emotional disturbance; on top of the normal cultural and other adjustment problems associated with a sudden move to an entirely new environment. The response of the Authorities was not one of addressing their difficulties and needs, but of branding many of them as "educationally subnormal," and then dispatching them to ESN schools."* By Bernard Coard.

   For more information about this read Bernard Coard's expose on this in his "*How the West Indian Child Is Made Educationally Subnormal in the British School System: The Scandal of the Black Child in Schools in Britain.* New Beacon for the Caribbean Education and Community Workers' Association; First Edition (6 May 1971). Also see his article entitled: "W*hy I Wrote the Book*" in The Guardian Newspaper *(2005).*

3. **GCE** – **General Certificate of Education** – The was an academic qualification that examination boards in the UK and a few of the former British colonies or Commonwealth countries conferred on children age of 16; end of their compulsory schooling. **GCE** is compared with **CSE** (**Certificate of Secondary Education**), which came later. ***Achieving CSE grade 1 was equivalent to achieving an GCE Ordinary level in the subject.***
4. **CSE** was an academic qualification awarded between 1965 and 1987 in England, Wales, and Northern Ireland. CSE was introduced to provide a qualification available to all schoolchildren distinct from the GCE exams, aimed at the more able pupils, mostly those at grammar and independent, (not the secondary modern schools), aiming for places at a university.

5. The Works of Sigmund Freud, Carl Jung and Michel Foucault
6. Said, Edward: (1978) ***Orientalism***. New York: Pantheon Books

\+ ***Men of Harlech*** Song: It would seem that 'this stirring music first appeared as *March of the Men of Harlech* in Musical and Poetical Relics of the Welsh Bards (Edward Jones, London 1784). The song was also used in the movie "*Zulu*"(1964).

Photo Credits & Acknowledgements:

The Author and Publisher would like to acknowledge use of photos by Courtesy of the following:

- *Lord Kitchener* (Theophilus London) – **tntisland.com**
- *De Fosto* (Winston Scarborough): **www.panonthenet.com**
- *Bro. Valentino* (Ellord Phillip): **www.pinterest.com**
- *Singing Sandra* (Sandra DesVignes-Millington): **cropoverbarbados.com**
- *The Mighty Striker* (Percy Oblington): **www.trinidadandtobagonews**
- *The Mighty Shadow* (Winston Anthony Bailey OBE): *David Rudder* - **www.socafreak.com**
- *Aaron Duncan:-All Rounder*: **-www.guardian.co.uk**
- *Lord Kitchener* (Aldwyn Roberts): Keith "Keithos" Anderson, Trinidad Guardian **www.tntisland.com**
- *Calypso Rose* (Martha Linda Sandy-Lewis): **www.caribbeaubelle.com**
- *The Mighty Sparrow* (Francisco Slinger): **www.mightysparrow.com**
- *Albert M Gomes: - Lingo: - Pink Panther:* – **Guardian.co.tt**
- *Lord Pretender, Brother Resistance* – **www.nctt**
- *Black Prince: – Black Stalin:* - **www.tucott.com**
- *Lord Nelson*: – *Tigress:* - *Sugar Aloes*: - **www.newsday.co.tt**
- *Duane O'Connor*: - **www.jayblessed.com**
- *Caribbean Fruit:* **www.caribbeanamericanweekly**
- *Sample of food from the Caribbean*: **www.tripadvisor.com**
- Map of Grenada: **http://www.lib.utexas.edu/maps/americas.htm**
- *St. Georges Market, St. Georges*: **grenadaexplorer.com**

The Series Editor and Author

Roselle Thompson, the series Editor and Author, has been a Head Teacher at both Primary and Secondary Schools and A Research Assistant in Caribbean Studies at the University of North London (Now *London Metropolitan University*), where she lectured in the UK. She has also been an Assistant Examiner in English Language, for one of the UK's major Examination Boards. Roselle is also a Poet, Broadcaster and International Speaker.

This Guide is an invaluable reading companion to help you understand ***A Woman of Destiny: A Calypso Novel***. It is packed with information on **Context, Plot, Structure, Diaspora, Style, Characters and Themes.**

Other Features:

- A Contextual Background
- Chapter Summaries
- Chapter Analyses
- Key Facts
- Significance of the Calypso
- Meaning of the Novel title
- Men & Destiny

For Orders:

Eagle Publications, **P O Box 73374, London W3 3FZ**

Tel: 07739 655 603 or 07848-844-377
E-mail: eaglepublications58@gmail.com

Lines are open 9am – 5pm: Monday to Saturday.

Website:www.eaglepublications.co.uk

Other Phoenix Study Guides in the Series written by the Author:

- ***English Grammar: A Student's Companion***
- ***Vocabulary Skills for Students & Teachers: A Practical Toolkit***
- ***Spelling & Word-power s Skills***
- ***Mastering Comprehension Skills***
- ***The New Caribbean Folktales & Legends for the 21st Century***
- ***Rhythms of Life: An Anthology of Modern Poetry***